THE ROLE OF THE JUVENILE POLICE IN THE

PROTECTION OF NEGLECTED AND

ABUSED CHILDREN

by

Vrinda Sharma Knapp

A Dissertation

DOCTOR OF SOCIAL WORK

FACULTY OF THE SCHOOL OF SOCIAL WORK

UNIVERSITY OF SOUTHERN CALIFORNIA

1961

REPRINTED IN 1975 BY

R AND E RESEARCH ASSOCIATES
4843 MISSION STREET, SAN FRANCISCO 94112
18581 McFARLAND AVENUE, SARATOGA, CA 95070

PUBLISHERS AND DISTRIBUTOR OF ETHNIC STUDIES
EDITOR: ADAM S. ETEROVICH
PUBLISHER: ROBERD D. REED

LIBRARY OF CONGRESS CARD CATALOG NUMBER

74-29574

ISBN

0-88247-320-4

TABLE OF CONTENTS

LIST OF TABLES

CHAPTER I

INTRODUCTION

This is a study of the role of juvenile police in the protection of children who are the victims of adult neglect and abuse in one geographic area of a metropolitan city. Its focus is on the activities of the juvenile police from the time a complaint of child neglect or abuse is brought to their attention until their responsibility ends.

The subject of neglect and abuse of children by parents and other adults receives frequent newspaper publicity in reports of the more sensational cases which occur. For example, the following are excerpts from news items published in the Los Angeles Times.

Child Neglect Charge Jails Van Nuys Couple

Officers went to the C. home on complaint of a neighbor who said the children were rummaging through garbage cans to find somethint to eat. The neighbor also said that the youngsters had been missing school because they had no clean clothes to wear. The children were identified as L. 10, W. 9, A. 8, B. 4, and A. 3, . . . The couple's home was cluttered with dirty dishes, stale food, empty cans and unwashed laundry. They were arrested for allegedly endangering the lives of their five children. . .[1]

Mother of 7 Arrested Again on Child Charge

Six children ranging in age from two months to sixteen years were taken from their home early yesterday by juvenile police officers and their mother was booked on suspicion of endangering the lives of children by ne-glect. Officers said the house was unkempt, did not have a stove and was littered with refuse. The children, with the exception of a sixteen year old firl, were dirty and wearing soiled clothing. A seventh child, a 14 year old girl, had been missing since September 13. The mother, Mrs. R., 34, was asleep when the officers arrived. Mrs. R was on probation from a previous conviction of endangering the lives of . . .[2]

Most neglect cases, however, do not receive newspaper coverage, and information concerning them remains in the files of the police and welfare agencies.

The two cases illustrated above, and most other child neglect and abuse cases which appear in newspapers, indicate the presence of police. The importance of juvenile police in safeguarding the child in these situations is common knowledge; yet, despite this fact, no systematic study of the role of juvenile police in the protection of such children has been made.[3]

It is hoped that the present study may be helpful to social workers, not only in understanding the specific responsibilities of the juvenile police in child neglect and abuse cases but also in becoming informed about the kinds of such cases which come to police attention, the various factors which help juvenile police to decide on the disposition of these cases, and some of the problems which they have when protective and other child welfare services in the community are inadequate.

Police are the primary agents of the local and state governments responsible by law for the protection of life and property and maintenance of law and order. To carry out this responsibility they have authority over persons of all ages, children and adults alike. The juvenile police divisions, wherever they exist, have, among other functions, the specific responsibility of protecting neglected and abused children.[4]

Legislative provisions, giving the state governments the right to protect the neglected and abused children, are found in all the states. In the State of California, most actions which the police take on behalf of the neglected child are under the provisions of the Welfare and Institutions Code in Sections 700a, 700b, 700c, and 700d.[5] The Penal Code of the State of California, in Sections 273a and 273d, makes provision for protecting children from "wilful cruelty or unjustifiable punishment . . . endangering life or health and physical abuse, immoral and vicious acts by adults in the presence of children."[6] Any adult responsible for any of the above acts toward a child is guilty of a misdemeanor or a felony.

The philosophy of the two codes, however, is quite different. The Welfare and Institutions Code focuses its concern on the welfare of the child and his family and keeping the family together in so far as possible. The Penal Code, on the other hand, aims at punitive retribution of crime. In any case of neglect or abuse of children, therefore, the police are often forced into the dual responsibility of adult punishment and child protection.

In spite of the vital role which police have in this program, child welfare and protective agencies have made little effort to understand the function of the police or to recognize them as an important part of the team which cares for the welfare of all children. A survey of the child welfare literature reveals that, while the role of the juvenile police has been adequately recognized with reference to the problem of juvenile delinquency, their role in the area of child protection has been relatively unnoticed.

This attitude of indifference is understandable to some extent, if we look at the present situation against the background of the early child protective agencies of the nineteenth century which functioned with "police power" and had strictly an "arm of the law" approach, both toward the neglected and abused children and their offending parents. This approach was acceptable at that time because the child protective movement had a legalistic birth. The program was given life by the passage of laws and was nurtured by those who enforced these laws. But gradually, over a period of time, as the practice of social work developed and new knowledge and understanding changed the philosophy of child welfare, the protective and child welfare agencies moved farther and farther away from the idea of law enforcement as the only method of protecting children. Police and law enforcement became symbolic of "authority" and an approach which focused only on the prosecution and punishment of parents. The casework method of helping the parents who neglected their children viewed the authoritarian or the punitive approach with distaste.

However, additional knowledge and experience in casework has gradually caused social workers to develop a positive approach toward the use of authority. Today, authority is recognized to be inherent in the very role of the social worker in relation to the client. It is believed that:

> Every casework relationship starts with a formal authority relationship . . . In each case, in any social agency, the formal authority relationship must become a relationship fo psychological authority if the client is to be helped. In the casework relationship, whenever the psychological aspect of authority relation develops strongly, the formal social authority aspects, although still present and effective, become secondary.[7]

Some of the existing child welfare agencies offering protective service, while focusing on the rehabilitation of the home, also have some degree of legal authority which makes it possible for them not only to use aggressive casework techniques but also to invoke the authority of a juvenile court in cases where it becomes necessary.[8]

The law enforcement philosophy and techniques pertaining to children have also changed considerably during the last sixty years, after the passage of the first state juvenile court law in this country. Since then legislation covering police activity with juveniles has focused more and more on "protection" and "rehabilitation." For example, a conference sponsored by the Children's Bureau in cooperation with the International Association of the Chiefs of Police reports:

> If the will of the people as expressed in our laws is to be honored, police procedure governing the treatment of children should carry out the philosophy of protection and rehabilitation. Otherwise the entire effort of a community to redeem and protect its youth may be wrecked and nullified at the very outset.[9]

The same report discussing the services of police with reference to the neglected children emphasizes that:

> In dealing with neglected children the police should bear in mind society's long term objective: The re-establishment of the home. The disposition made should therefore be in accord with this objective.[10]

Police departments in most urban cities and counties now have either special juvenile units or appoint trained officers specialized in work with children. In the findings of a Special Juvenile Delinquency Project-International Association of Chiefs of Police query, 50 percent of the communities covered reported that they had special officers on the police force for work with juveniles.[11] The importance of training officers in juvenile work, both before and after their selection, is also being recognized more and more by the police departments. Efforts are made to select persons for juvenile work from within the police force, who have shown aptitude and ability to work, with warmth and understanding, with children and their parents in trouble.

Today, the objective of both types of agencies, those working within the framework of child welfare as well as those working within the framework of law enforcement, with regard to the neglected and abused children can be the same: protection of such children and rehabilitation of their home. It, therefore, becomes necessary that each understand the role of the other, so as to be able to complement and supplement each other's function in their joint venture.

As stated earlier, the focus of this study is on the role of the juvenile police in protecting children who are neglected and abused. In the following pages there is a brief discussion of the concept of "role," followed by the purpose, scope, and method of the study.

The Concept of Role

Much has been written about the concept of "role" in the last forty years. Within their own discipline, sociologists, cultural anthropologists, and social psychologists have developed this concept and defined it in various ways. Students of the social sciences make use of it frequently when analyzing the structure and functioning of social systems as well as when explaining individual behavior. It, therefore, becomes necessary here to clarify and define role as it is used in this study.

An extensive yet concise review of social science literature, published between 1900-1950, pertaining to the definition and analysis of the concept of role, was made by L. J. Neiman and J. W. Huges.[12] In an attempt to systematize the wide variety of definitions, usages and implications of this concept which the authors came across, they were grouped under three broad headings: (1) definitions which use role to describe the dynamic process of personality development; (2) definitions in terms of society as a whole; and (3) definitions in terms of specific groups within the society.[13] This indeed is a very broad classification and even a cursory survey of literature on the subject reveals that different points of view and emphasis are given to this concept within a single discipline. Some individual authors have defined and used the concept differently over a period of time. It is outside the scope of this study to discuss in detail some of these differences or bring out the semantic problems that students of role-analysis must face. However, in the following paragraphs a few selected definitions from the social science literature are quoted to illustrate the differences in the emphasis and points of view of their authors.

Many anthropologists and sociologists, in defining "role," have acknowledged their indebtedness to two of Ralph Linton's works, The Study of Man[14] and The Cultural Background of Personality.[15] In these books he has developed the concept of "role" in association with the concept of "status" and this particular association is found most frequently in social science literature. In his earlier writings he stated:

> A role represents the dynamic aspects of a status. The individual is socially assigned to a status and occupies it with relation to other statuses. When he puts the rights and duties which constitute the status into effect, he is performing a role. Role and status are quite inseparable and the distinction between them is of only academic interest. There are no roles without statuses or statuses without role.[16]

Linton points out here that role and status are inseparable and in his later writings he reaffirms this interpretation, but adds:

> Every status is linked with a particular role, but the two things are by no means the same from the point of view of the individual. In so far as it represents overt behavior, a role is the dynamic aspect of a status . . .[17]

Commenting on Linton's definitions, a group of writers state:

> Role apparently has reference not to actual behavior of an occupant of a position but to behavioral standards . . . The definitions of a number of other authors fall in this 'normative cultural pattern' category.[18]

Talcott Parsons in some of his writings has defined role with a similar emphasis. In one of his essays on "Position and Prospects of Systematic Theory in Sociology" he wrote:

> From the point of view of the social system, a role is an element of generalized patterning of the action of its component individuals . . . From the point of view of the actor his role is defined by the normative expectations of the members of the group as formulated in its social traditions.[19]

A few years later, in his essay on "Psychoanlysis and the Social Structure," he pointed out:

> In this context what is meant by social structure is a system of patterned expectations of the behavior of individuals who occupy particular statuses in the social system. Such a system of patterned legitimate expectations is called by sociologists a system of roles.[20]

Some sociologists and social psychologists like Florian Znaniecki,[21] Kimball Young,[22] Robert L. Sutherland and Julian L. Woodword[23] have defined role with somewhat similar points of view.

A few writers have focused on role in relation to some aspects of personality development. Leonard S. Cottrell in one of his earlier writings states:

Personality or the most significant part of it, is, the organization of the roles a person plays in group life . . . The role is the organization of habits and attitudes of the individual appropriate to a given position in a system of social relationships.[24,]

Gardner Murphy, discussing the cultural phase of personality, says:

It is not to culture as a whole but to specific roles, that the cultural phase of personality owes its origin. Roles in terms of age, sex, occupation, etc. are assigned to the child and through such serially enacted roles, as through a tube, he makes his way to old age. Personality is, in considerable degree, a matter of role behavior; even more, however, it is a matter of role perception and of self perception in the light of the role.[25]

Norman Cameron states:

In our discussion of personality development we saw that social roles are organized and differentiated quite early in life . . . we mean by role, a comprehensive and coherent organization in behavior of functionally related interlocking attitudes and responses . . . In real life situations, role taking means earnestly behaving as, and therefore actually being, a particular social person in relation to other persons.[26]

Yet other social scientists have defined role with emphasis on the behavior of the persons occupying social positions. They do not refer to what the individuals occupying these positions should do, but what they actually do. Kingsley Davis's definition falls in this category. He says:

A position whether status or office defines a minimum of obligatory behavior for the incumbent but it cannot insure that the incumbent will carry out this behavior perfectly. . . . The role then is the manner in which a person actually carries out the requirements of his position.[27]

Theodore Newcomb, on the other hand, makes a different between roles and role behaviors. He states:

A role consists of a whole set of behaviors which are more or less characteristic of all occupants of a position . . . Role and prescribed-roles, therefore, are not concepts which refer to actual behavior of any given individual . . . . Role behavior on the other hand does refer to the actual behavior of specific individuals as they take roles.[28]

Theordore Sarbin has a similar point of view:

Role enactments are the overt performances of persons; these performances validate or invalidate the expectations of the other persons or persons in a social situation.[29]

These selected definitions give a general idea of how social scientists have defined and used the concept of role. The definitions also indicate that most authors believe that people do not behave in a random manner but that behavior of most individuals is influenced by their own expectations or the expectation of others in the group or of the society in which they live.

For the purpose of this study Kingsley Davis's definition[30] of role seems most suitable. Unlike some social scientiest who have defined role with reference to "behavioral standards," "normative expectations of the members of the group" or "patterned expectations of the behavior of individuals," his emphasis is on the "actual behavior" of the occupants of a role. ". . . the role then is the manner in which a person actually carries out the requirements of his position." While it is not proposed to adopt his definition word for word for this study, the concept "role" is used here to encompass the idea emphasized in his definition. This study will focus on the activities of the juvenile police, who are law enforcement agents, as they actually carry out the responsibility of protecting neglected and abused children.

Purpose of the Study

The overall objective of this study is to acquire a better understanding of the methods, responsibilities, and problems of the juvenile police in handling cases of neglected and abused children.

More fundamentally, this dissertation has the objective of inquiring into the method of operation of the juvenile police and their reasons for operating either under the Welfare and Institutions Code or the Penal Code, in any given situation of child neglect and abuse. This is important because the philosophy of the two codes is very different.

In order to understand the overall role of the juvenile police in the protection of neglected and abused children, the study has the additional purpose of clarifying the specific factors in neglect and abuse cases, which help juvenile police to decide upon the various sections of the two codes under which to operate. It would be pertinent to explore those cases which could possibly present a conflict as to the choice of code, to discover which code is given preference and the reasons for this preference.

While the juvenile police have the specific responsibility of protecting children from the immediate situation of neglect and abuse, they are not a protective agency with rehabilitation of the family as their main objective. The community provides protective and other child welfare services to carry out this function. However, many communities, including Los Angeles,[31] do not have adequate services in this area. This study is to look into the problems which the juvenile police have in the absence of adequate protective services in a community.

In order to understand the role, responsibilities, and limits of the juvenile police in the field of child protection, the following questions were formulated for exploration, with reference to 100 cases os child neglect and abuse handled by the juvenile police, in one area of the metropolitan city of Los Angeles in the year 1958.

Question One

What is the role of the juvenile police in the protection of the neglected and abused children?

The concept "role" is used here to mean the "actual performance" of the juvenile police, who are law enforcement agents, in protecting children who are neglected and abused by adults. The focus is on the step-by-step activities of the juvenile police from the time they receive a complaint or detect a case of child neglect and abuse until they terminate their contact with the case.

Question Two

What are the specific factors in situations of child neglect and abuse which help the juvenile police to decide whether they will operate under the Welfare and Institutions Code or the Penal Code? Does conflict arise when a case can be handled under either code? The study explores these questions with the help of case illustrations and analysis of police activity in these cases.

Question Three

What are the problems encountered by juvenile police in handling complaints of neglected and abused children, when protective services are nonexistent or inadequate in a community?

Available facts and figures reveal that protective services offered to children by the public and private agencies are not adequate in many communities in the United States.[32] The juvenile police responsibilities in these communities become complex because they are essentially a law enforcement agency, not a rehabilitative agency, and they perform the service of child protection without the aid of rehabilitation facilities. This study explores some of the major problems which juvenile police have in one such community.

Method of the Study

The preceding questions are explored in this study with the help of an analysis of 100 cases of neglect and abuse. The analysis is supplemented with opinions of juvenile officers who handled these cases, secured through individual interviews and discussions with them. It is further supplemented with information gathered by observing their actual work on some cases of child neglect and abuse, visiting agencies such as the probation department, Juvenile Hall, juvenile and adult courts. Information about the training and selection of the juvenile police is given briefly and was obtained by studying the training program and visiting the police academy.

Selection of Locale

Before selecting cases for analysis, it was necessary to select a geographic area. In consultation with the lieutenant in charge of the juvenile police headquarters in Los Angeles, it was decided to select the cases from the Central Division, which is one of the fourteen divisions of the city.[33] This division includes Hoover Street on the west, Los Angeles River on the north and east, and Pico Boulevard on the south. According to the information available through the Planning and Research Division of the Los Angeles Police Department this area had a total population of about 161,000 in 1956, of which about 7,000 were Negroes.

Selection of Cases

In the selection of cases the following factors had to be kept in mind. In the first place, it was necessary to select only the completed cases, so that police activity could be studied in each case from start to finish. Second, it was important to select cases which were handled by those officers who would be available for interviews and discussions of their cases; and third, it was desirable not to select cases that were more than a year old in order ot maximize the accuracy and detail obtainable from the police officers about these cases.

Keeping these points in mind, it was decided to select cases from the year 1958 (the data were collected in 1959). The Central Division had registered 137 cases of child neglect and 88 cases of child abuse during this year. This made a total of 225 cases. In the group of 88 cases classified under abuse, there were 16 "no action" cases. This meant that, while a complaint was registered, no action could be taken by the juvenile police for prosecuting the offender, either for lack of evidence or inability on the part of the victim to identify the offender. It was decided to delete these cases from the group of abuse cases. This narrowed down the universe to a total of 209 cases, approximately 65 percent of the total being neglect cases and 35 percent abuse cases.

Each of the 209 cases was studied in order to gain knowledge of the range of material involved and the nature of the problem of making a detailed study. The names of the police officers responsible for each case were noted for determination of availability for interview. Subsequent inquiry showed that the officers who were readily available accounted for less than 50 percent of the 209 cases, or somewhat less than 100 cases. The other officers were either on leave, transferred to other districts, or retired. A preliminary investigation indicated that for an adequately detailed study of each case, including an interview with the officer concerned, about 100 cases would represent a reasonable limit. An examination of the cases of the available officers showed that they fell into approximately the same ratio for neglect and abuse as did the 209 in the original universe. The cases for which all information could be made available were therefore representative of all the cases, in so far as the neglect and abuse ratio is concerned, and they represented a number which was just within the range of manageability for the study concerned. It was therefore decided to use the cases of only the available officers for the purposes of this study.

This may be regarded as an expedient sampling of the 209 cases which is coincidentally a purposive or representative sampling, but it is in fact a 100 percent sampling of all cases for which all facts were readily available.

During the course of the study, however, it was noted that duplication of circumstances and data was sometimes involved where, for example, one adult might abuse six children leading to six more or less identical complaints with but different names on each. From such groups of cases it was decided to use just one case in order that one adult should not unduly influence final results. During the course of the interviews it was also learned that one or two of the non-available officers could possibly become available through personal contacts. A decision was therefore made to expand the universe of cases for which all facts were available and a goal of 100 cases was established as an objective. The newly available officers were reached in retirement or in other divisions of the police force, but the effort involved precluded the feasibility of any further expansion of the universe of available cases. The one hundredth case represented the limit of availability and feasibility.

The Schedule

The selected cases were studied from the juvenile police records and the relevant information was transferred to a schedule (Appendix B).

The first part of the schedule was to gather factual information such as the name, address, age, sex, and racial background of the children and their parents, the nature of complaint, the section of code under which the case was booked, and the final disposition of the case.

The second part of the schedule was to help gather information about the source and method of complaint and the investigation procedure of the juvenile police. Questions in this part were focused on finding out the persons contacted during the investigation besides the parents and the method by which evidence of neglect was established, whether or not the children in the case were questioned about their neglect conditions, their reaction and the parents' reaction to the investigation. It was not possible to obtain the children's reaction accurately in most cases because unless a child had been unusually upset or frightened, the officers did not record his reactions. Similarly, parents' reaction to their investigation is not recorded in all cases.

The third part of the schedule referred to the type of decisions made by the juvenile police regarding the neglected and abused children and their parents, the specific factors in the situation which helped them to make their decision, and the reaction of the children and parents to that decision. Here again, the reactions of the children and parents were not a matter of record and hence could not be used in the study.

The fourth part of the schedule dealt with the execution of the decision regarding the children and their parents. The main focus was to find out the way children were handled, particularly when the decision was to remove them to Juvenile Hall, and the responsibility of the juvenile police after taking the children to Juvenile Hall.

The last part of the schedule was to obtain the juvenile officer's opinion on whether the case was an isolated or chronic case of neglect, the reason why some parents neglect and abuse their children, their role in protecting children in the community as they visualize it, and the availability and use of other child welfare agencies in the community.

Interviews with the Juvenile Police Officers

The twelve officers who handled the 100 cases under study were interviewed and the cases were discussed. These interviews proved very helpful because most officers keep informal records on cases which they handle. These informal records include not only the important factual information about a case but also information which need not necessarily go onto formal records, such as detail of advise or warning given to a family, or significant remarks made by a child. The focus of these interviews was on the officer's activities in each case. Their individual opinions were invited about the problem of neglect and abuse of children as they see it and their role in handling it as law enforcement officers.

Observation of Actual Handing of Neglect and Abuse Cases

One of the many protective aspects of the juvenile police program in Los Angeles is their night patrol system. Juvenile police officers in plain clothes and unmarked cars cruise in the city between the hours of 4:30 p.m. and 1:15 a.m. To observe this activity three evenings, spread over a period of one month, were spent cruising with juvenile officers on their night patrol. This helped in acquiring first-hand knowledge of the patrol as a method of detecting as well as correcting neglect and abuse situations.

To observe actual situations of neglect and abuse after they were reported to the police, three cases, two of child neglect and one of child beating, were visited with the police. This helped in obtaining a better understanding of some situations of neglect, the reactions of the parents and children when confronted by police, and the method of investigation of the police.

Visits to Agencies

Agencies with which the juvenile police work for the disposition of the neglect and abuse cases were visited along with the juvenile police officers. These were (1) Juvenile

Hall, where the neglected and abused children are housed, temporarily, after juvenile police take them into custody; (2) the area office of the Los Angeles County Probation Department with whom the juvenile police work closely (It is on the basis of facts presented by the juvenile police, about a particular case of neglect or abuse, that the Probation Department starts its investigation. Much information is exchanged and consultation completed between the personnel of the two departments concerning cases referred by the juvenile police. The working of the Probation Department was discussed in detail with one of the deputy probation officers); (3) proceedings of both the Juvenile Court and the Adult Court were observed to understand the juvenile police role after the cases are referred to these courts.

Training and Selection of the Juvenile Police

Performance of any group of people can best be understood when one has knowledge about the type of training they have and the structure and function of the agency in which they work. The general training program for the police was studied by visiting the police academy, and the various aspects of the program were discussed with the director of the academy. The screening and selection procedure of the juvenile police officers was discussed in detail with the lieutenant in charge of the selection. The general structure and functions of the juvenile police units were discussed with officers concerned, supplemented by studying the relevant parts of the Juvenile Police Manual.

The data thus collected were used as the primary source of information. The secondary source of information has been the review of the available literature, both for securing the historical facts and for supporting and supplementing discussions in the study.

Nature of the Report

The following five chapters discuss the different aspects of this study. The next chapter (Chapter II) gives a historical account of the development of protective services in the United States. An attempt is made to show how the development of other child welfare programs and the practice of social casework had its impact on protective services.

Chapter III discusses in general, the development of the juvenile police in the United States, with special reference to Los Angeles.

Chapters IV and V analyze the 100 cases of neglect and abuse respectively, the main focus being on the police role in handling these cases. Representative situations of neglect and abuse of children are illustrated and police activity is described. The methods by which these cases are brought to the attention of the juvenile police, their method of investigation, the factors important in their decision making, and final disposition of the cases are topics discussed in these chapters.

Chapter VI discusses the findings of the two previous chapters concerning the actual police role in the protection of children in a community. The implications of the findings as well as some suggestions for closer cooperation between the juvenile police and child welfare agencies in the protection of children are given.

Footnotes

[1] Los Angeles Times, September 12, 1959, p. 2.

[2] Ibid., October 15, 1959, p. 3.

[3] Alice Hamlett and Joan Overturf, "Protective Service of the Police" (unpublished Master's thesis, University of Southern California, 1958). This is an analysis of six child beating and six unfit home cases which were handled by the juvenile police.

[4] John P. Kenney and Dan G. Pursuit, Police Work With Juveniles (Springfield, Illinois: Charles C. Thomas, 1954), p. 19.

[5] Welfare and Institutions Code and Laws Relating to Social Welfare--State of California (Sacramento: Printing Division, Document Section, 1957), Section 700, p. 119. (Appendix A)

[6] Deering's Penal Code of the State of California (San Francisco: Bancroft-Whitney Company, 1949), p. 109. (Appendix A)

[7] Elliot Studt, "An Outline for Study of Social Authority Factors in Casework," Child Welfare, June 1954, p. 233.

[8] Vincent Defrancis, The Fundamentals of Child Protection (Denver: Children's Division, The American Humane Association, 1955), pp. 8-9.

[9] Children's Bureau, Publication Number 334, Police Services for Juveniles (Washington: U. S. Government Printing Office, 1954), p. 5.

[10] Ibid., p. 34.

[11] Ibid., p. 38.

[12] Lionel J. Neiman and James W. Huges, "The Problem of the Concept of Role," Social Forces, December 1951, pp. 141-149.

[13] Ibid., p. 143.

[14] Ralph Linton, The Study of Man (New York: Appleton-Century Co., 1936).

[15] Ralph Linton, The Cultural Background of Personality (New York: Appleton-Century Co., 1945).

[16] Linton, The Study of Man, p. 114.

[17] Linton, The Cultural Background of Personality, p. 78.

[18] N. Gross, W. S. Mason, and A. W. McEachern, Explorations in Role Analysis (New York: John Wiley and Sons Inc., 1958), p. 12.

[19] Talcott Parsons, Essays in Sociological Theory (Illinois: The Free Press, 1954), p. 230.

[20] Ibid., p. 337.

[21] Florian Znaniecki, The Social Role of Man of Knowledge (New York: Columbia University Press, 1940), p. 19.

[22] Kimball Young, Social Psychology (New York: Appleton Century, 1956), p. 88.

[23] Robert L. Sutherland and Julian L. Woodword, Introductory Sociology (New York: Lippincott, 1940), pp. 250-53.

[24] Leonard S. Cottrell, "Roles and Marital Adjustments," American Sociological Review, May 1933, pp. 107, 112.

[25] Gardner Murphy, Personality--A Biosocial Approach to Origins and Structure (New York: Harper and Brothers, 1947), pp. 559-560.

[26] Norman Cameron, The Psychology of Behavior Disorders (Boston: Houghton Mifflin Company, 1947), pp. 89-90.

[27] Kingsley Davis, Human Society (New York: Macmillan Co., 1949), pp. 89-90.

[28] Theordore M. Newcomb, Social Psychology (New York: The Dryden Press, 1950), p. 330.

[29] Theodore R. Sarbin, "Role Theory," in Handbook of Social Psychology, Vol. I, ed. Gardner Lindzey (Cambridge: Addison Wesley Co., 1954), p. 224.

[30] Davis, op.cit., pp. 89-90.

[31] Welfare Planning Council, Los Angeles Region, A Protective Services Program (Los Angeles: Welfare Planning Council, 1956), p. 3.

[32] Vincent Defrancis, Child Protective Services in the United States--A Nationwide Survey (Denver: Children's Division, The American Humane Association, 1956).

[33] Since the time of this study the number of geographic divisions has increased to fifteen.

CHAPTER II

A BRIEF HISTORY OF CHILD PROTECTION

IN THE UNITED STATES

In this chapter the history of child protection in the United States is discussed briefly, highlighting the major events.

The Doctrine of Parens Patriae

Under the old Persian, Egyptian, Greek, Gallic, and Roman law, the father had absolute power over his children. Infanticide was lawful and the father could sell his sons and daughters into slavery. While generally speaking fathers loved their children and did not desire to kill them or sell them or rule them in an arbitrary or selfish way, they had the right to do so and the state enforced these rights instead of interceding on behalf of the child.[1]

Under English Common Law, which was the basis of American Law, the father had supreme control over his legitimate minor children and was entitled to the custody of his children. The law paid little regard to the rights of the mother or the interest of the child.[2] Most rights in society are accompanied by obligations and, under the Common Law, while the father had the control and custody of his children, he also had the obligation to support and protect the children. However, in the early Middle Ages, this obligation was purely a moral one and for a long time was not legally enforceable.

The father's authority in the family, or the doctrine of "pater potestas" of Roman times, had often been questioned, but it was not until the Middle Ages that the state began to acquire the legal right to usurp the father's authority.

The first restrictions on these absolute rights of the father came from the Court of Chancery. The Middle Ages vacillated between two opinions and took some time to decide whether guardianship was a valuable right existing solely for the advantage of the guardian or whether it also involved responsibilities toward the infant.[3]

It was felt that if the father can enforce his rights, his duties should also be enforceable. As a result of social change and changes in the conception of the rights and duties of a guardian, many a father found himself sharing his authority over a child with the state.

The right of the state to act on behalf of or in the welfare of the child, even if it means depriving the natural or legal parent of his control and custody of the child, is referred to as the doctrine of _Parens Patriae._ The fundamental assumption in the doctrine is the right of the state to assume responsibility toward the well being of children when needed.

The King as _Parens Patriae_ became the guardian when required of wards who had no one to protect their interests; and exercising his power through the Lord Chancellor and later through the Court of Chancery, gradually came to inquire into the way in which all guardians were fulfilling their trust. Thus it became possible for children to be made wards of courts more properly known as wards of chancery.[4]

Once the child came under the protection of the state or became a "ward of court" then the court had a right to inquire into all the circumstances of the case for the protection and welfare of the ward. The court could also interfere in cases where it was found that the parents were immoral or otherwise unfit to take care of their children. It could therefore interfere if a child was being treated with cruelty or if an unsuitable marriage was being arranged for the child. In such instances the parent's right of custody was taken over by the court and the child's welfare was looked into. If the child was old enough to choose for himself then his wishes were given consideration.

The Common Law in England was also challenged when it was realized that its approach was unjust to the mother since she had no right over her child. Gradually, as the importance of the welfare of children was established, the mother's rights could not be ignored and parental rights became more nearly equal. As the community gained the increasing right to interfere with parents who were unable to meet their obligations toward their children, parental responsibilities came to be defined and parents' duty to maintain, educate, and protect their children became enforceable by law.

The American Scene

Although the roots of American Law are to be found in English Common Law, the absoluteness of a father's control over the child, as was observed in England, did not exist here. In the earlier periods in the colonies, while the courts gave primary custody of the child to the father, the mother's rights as well as the child's welfare were not entirely overlooked.[5] This was so because women in this country were accorded a larger measure of equality with men, as they struggled by the side of men to develop a new country. Furthermore, this country's rebellion against the control and domination by England naturally carried with it the desire not to adopt practices which existed in England, and which the settlers felt were undesirable or unfair.

The doctrine of <u>Parens Patriae</u> in the United States is found in laws formulated as early as the eighteenth century for the protection of children.

Numerous instances are found in the statutes of various states from 1790-1825, authorizing the binding out or commitment to almhouses of children found begging on the street or whose parents were beggars . . . From about 1825 there came a more and more general recognition and practical application of the principle that it is the right and duty of the public authorities to intervene in cases of parental cruelty or gross neglect seriously endangering the health, morals, or elementary education of children and to remove the children by force if necessary, and place them under surroundings more favorable for their development.[6]

In spite of such provisions made in the statutes of the time, there is little evidence on record that these laws were put into operation effectively.

The class of children who are now forcibly removed from the control of unfit parents apparently remained with their families, as a rule, until the latter became destitute, when the children were cared for as pauper children or until the fruits of neglect were reaped and the children, convicted of offenses, were sent to jails and penitentiaries along with older offenders.[7]

However, with the passage of time, the child protection laws in the various states were made more definite and clear and the courts gradually became less hesitant to exercise their power to remove the child from the custody of its parents, when that was found to be necessary.

In 1840 Senator Paige, in discussing a case before the New York Supreme Court, said:

By the law of nature the father has no paramount right of the custody of his child. By that law the wife and child are equal to the husband and father, but inferior and subject to their sovereign. The head of a family, in his character of husband and father, has no authority over his wife and children; but in his character of sovereign he has. On the establishment of Civil Societies, the power of the chief of a family as sovereign passes to the chief or government of the nation. And that chief or magistrate of the nation not possessing the requisite knowledge necessary to a judicious discharge of the duties of guardianship and education of children, such portion of the sovereign power as relates to the discharge of these duties is transferred to the parents, subject to such restrictions and limitations as sovereign power of the nation think proper to prescribe. There is no parental authority independent of the supreme power of the state. But the power is derived altogether from the latter. The moment a child is born, it owes allegiance to the government of the country of its birth and is entitled to the protection of that government. And such government is obliged to its duty of protection to consult the welfare, comfort and interest of such child in regulating its custody during the period of its minority. . .[8]

In spite of the earlier general awareness of states' rights over parents and the states' responsibility for protecting neglected and abused children, an organized movement for child protection did not develop until the end of the nineteenth century.

Contribution of the Humane Movement in Developing Child Protection Program

The Humane movement, first in England and later in this country, contributed a great deal toward the protection of children, even though welfare of the children was by no means its sole purpose. The word "Humane" refers to both animal and child protection. As is known from recorded facts, humanitarian concern in an organized form was expressed first for the animals and only later for children. Even when laws existed for the protection of children, the law enforcement agencies were hesitant to interfere between parents and their authority over their children. But an animal was a mute helpless creatur. If it were ill treated by human beings, it could not speak, defend itself, or escape the situation.

The first Humane legislation was passed in England in 1822 and was known as the Martin Act. Richard Martin secured "passage of this first statute from a legislative body, which recognized the duty of the prevention of cruelty to animals, not as an economic equation in life, but as a matter of conscience and conduct."[9] Following this act in 1824, the first English society for the prevention of cruelty to animals was organized in London. Its purpose was the spreading of humane education and making the enforcement of existing laws possible.

The first organized American society for the prevention of cruelty to animals was established in 1866, though cruelty to animals had been protested even in the colonial days. As early as 1640 the Massachusetts Body of Liberties made reference to cruelty to animals and in May 1775, a poem entitled "Cruelty to Animals Exposed" was published in a Pennsylvania magazine.[10] The name associated with starting the humane movement in this country is that of Henry Bergh. He was interested in prevention of cruelty to animals as well as children. His trip to England acquainted him with the work of the Royal Society for the Prevention of Cruelty to Animals in London and on his return to America he interested people in starting a similar society, which was incorporated by an act of the New York Legislature in April 1866.

The philosophy and ideas about the natural rights and of man and "rational humanitarianism" became a reality after the Declaration of Independence. The crusade against slavery, prison reforms, improvement of mental hospitals, etc. reflect clearly how the natural rights philosophy was put into practice. Yet, almost through the first half of the nineteenth century, there is no evidence of public attention being focused upon the problem of child neglect and cruelty. As noted earlier, there was some evidence of its awareness in the statutes. However, problems of slavery and other social problems were so overwhelming and urgent that other less overwhelming problems, like child abuse and neglect, were neglected for some time.

-18-

It is interested to note how the American Humane movement became interested in protecting children from cruelty in addition to animals. In 1874, eight years after the first law in New York was passed for the protection of animals, the case of a little girl by the name of Mary Ellen was brought to the attention of the community. It was found that this child was beaten daily by her stepmother and tormented in other cruel ways, her condition was very pathetic. However, when her case was taken up for protection, it was discovered that the child could have no protection under the law until the guilt of her persecutor was established under existing legal forms.[11] The American Society for the Prevention of Cruelty to Animals was therefore asked to handle the case. This case marked the beginning of the movement of protection of cruelty to children. Soon, other such cases were discovered in the community and the need to give protection to children from cruelty became evident. Hence a

> . . . society was formed to rescue children from vicious and immoral surroundings and to prosecute offenders, to prevent the cruel neglect, beating or abuse of children, to prevent the employment of children for mendicant purpose or in theatrical or acrobatic performances and for the enforcement of all laws for protection of minors from abuse.[12]

This first society in New York was followed by similar societies in Rochester, San Francisco, Philadelphia, Boston, Baltimore, and elsewhere, and within five years ten such societies were organized in various parts of the country.

Most of these societies followed the New York model and combined the work of child and animal protection together. Even though combining the work thus was criticized by many workers it was, in many instances, done more out of practical necessity than as a preference. These organizations being voluntary had limited financial or other resources, and in some instances this was a major limiting factor. However, some societies, such as the Colorado Bureau of Child and Animal Protection, also saw some value in combining these activities:

> The protection of children and the protection of animals are combined because the principle involved, i.e., their helplessness, is the same; because all life is the same, differing only in degree of development and expression and because each profit by association with the other.[13]

In the initial stages, the New York society remained aloof from all other children's agencies in New York and emphasized "child rescue," as a distinct phase of its work. The officers of this organization believed that societies for the prevention of cruelty to children were not created for the purpose of reforming or educating children or placing them in other homes. They believed that these societies are merely the "arm of law" whose function is to seize the child from unfit surroundings or from unfit parents, bring him to the court, and submit him to the decision of the court. Alternately, it should extend that "arm of Law" to those who are cruel to the children, bring them to the criminal court, and insure their prosecution and punishment. The New York society and others that followed tended to emphasize the separation of children from their families and the placement of children in reformatory and charitable institutions.[14]

On the other hand some of the other similar societies, such as the Pennsylvania and Massachusetts societies, were of the opinion, even in those days (1909), that the tendency of these societies to become "arms of the police" is dangerous. They regarded the anti-cruelty phase of the work as a diminishing one and felt the need for preventive and remedial measures instead.

> [They] recognized that the sanction of the law must often be invoked to promote the ends of the community and this is the distinctive function of anti-cruelty organizations; but in addition to the protection of children from bodily harm by this means and from serious neglect and moral injury, these societies must take upon themselves the work of developing conditions of normal family life . . . . The society has therefore a three fold task to perform. It must rescue children from degrading conditions, it must avail itself of every reasonable opportunity to try to reconstruct such families as are moving on the inevitable shipwreck and while it is working with each individual instance, it must try to seek out causes, which bring about these bad conditions, so it may do its part to prevent them. [15]

In spite of such opposing philosophies, the child protective phase of the Humane movement gathered momentum within a relatively short period, and by 1910 there were over 200 societies in the United States, [16] although most of these were patterned on the New York society's "arm of the law" plan. The one common objective on which they all agreed was the protection of the rights of childhood. However, they could not agree on the method which should be employed to protect these rights. Hence the movement lacked a common ideal and the necessary unifying force.

The Development of Other Child Welfare Programs and Their Effect on the Protective Program

The decades at the beginning of the twentieth century brought a new outlook and a new momentum not only in the area of child protection but in the field of child welfare as a whole. Several important events took place during and after this period and these were no doubt responsible for starting a new era in child welfare.

As Emma O. Lundberg describes it, the century of child began auspiciously. The first juvenile court had been established in 1899 and its coming into being reflected society's increasing awareness of the needs of its children. "It was the outgrowth of many years of steady effort on the part of individuals and organizations concerned with the protection of children." [17] The successful establishment of the first juvenile court was followed by a rapid development of children's courts throughout the country. [18] The second important event was the first White House Conference in 1909. This conference brought together a large number of people whose main interest and concern was the welfare of children. As a result of this conference an important concept emerged: "Homelife is the highest and finest product of civilization." This concept became an ideal and objective for many child welfare programs that followed. It was almost like an awakening to an idea, so basic to everything which concerned children's welfare. This concept was emphasized over and over again at the following White House Conferences as well as at other national and local child welfare conferences.

Following the first White House Conference and as a result of it, the United States Children's Bureau under the Department of Labor was set up in August 1912. This was another very important development; it was the first national organization of its kind and it became a clearing house for information regarding child welfare. The Bureau helped children's agencies with information and in many ways, and gave impetus to all types of child welfare work.

The development of Mother's Aid program (also known as the Mother's Pensions or Mother's Allowances) also gathered momentum after the first White House Conference. The much quoted stated of the 1909 White House Conference on dependent children undoubtedly influenced greatly the development of aid to children in their homes. [19]

These important events in a little more than a decade reflect the early twentieth century society's increasing awareness of the needs of children. However, while new ideas are born and principles expressed without much difficulty, their practical development and application involve changing the attitudes of people, especially those people who are concerned with the execution of the program incorporating the new ideas.

C. C. Carstens, Director of the Child Welfare League of America, wrote in 1921:

> The child protection movement alone of all specialities, seems to be a field full of division and controversy. The nature of its work is so vital to the maintenance of the family tie that the agencies of the movement have had to shape, definite, consistent and well thought out policies and to defend them vigorously. When the child is unable to get the proper protection in its own home, children's protective agencies have not hesitated to ask the court, as a last resort, to cut the family tie. This course is so abhorrent to certain people who do not realize the menace that a brutal parent or an immoral home may prove both to the child and the welfare of the community that it often becomes a subject of bitter legal and public controversy. [20]

In the same article Mr. Carstens further points out that these diverse philosophies by the agencies have naturally led to diverse practices also. The restrictionist group, considering themselves, first of all, agents for law enforcement, have recruited their paid personnel from the ranks of truant officers, deputy sheriffs, constables, or other public agents. [21]

However, the effects of the new programs and the changing philosophy of child welfare gradually had their effect on the conservative child protective societies. Their approach became less legalistic and less punitive as they recognized the value of rehabilitation and prevention in child protection. Needless to say, this change did not come overnight and the progressive societies deserve considerable credit for giving the lead to conservative societies in breaking away from old ideas.

While all this development and change was taking place in the field of child welfare, it is important to note that at the same time, social work as a profession was also gaining roots. The first few schools of social work had already come into existence in the first two decades of the twentieth century; this made it possible for some child welfare and protective agencies to employ trained workers, who could not only understand the goals of these programs but also had the skill for putting them into practice.

The period of World War I and the post war years affected all welfare programs considerably. Many private agencies were financially affected and as a result some sought increasing support from public funds while some others became inactive and had to close down. In the post war years, some of the protective societies started merging with children's aid societies. A few of the conservative societies at this time, much to the displeasure of the progressive societies, decided to join the humane association, which was primarily interested in the prevention of cruelty to animals.

Some of the child welfare agencies became interested in the preventive aspects of the protective program and in helping parents to understand and meet the needs of children. The agencies which added this activity to their existing program were the Children's Aid Societies, Family Welfare Societies, and the Juvenile Courts which were developing rapidly in the various states. Along with these, other agencies such as the Juvenile Protective Associations, Children's Aid Programs, Probation Services, and Police Women's Services also developed. The focus of all these services was directly and sometimes indirectly on child protection. Thus the responsibility of child protection was gradually being shared by several agencies.

The place of the juvenile court in relation to child protection needs special mention. In many states during this period juvenile courts did take a very active part in being an instrument of child protection. In the 1920's, many child welfare and other social welfare agencies felt that juvenile courts should take over the work of protective societies. However, leaders in the protective field felt differently:

> The children's protective functions of a juvenile court are inherent
> in the very structure and organization. In many instances it is doubtless
> the best instrument to use and in some instances, family reconstruction and
> child protection are impossible without recourse to some court. There are,
> however, many instances in which child life is menaced, which would either
> not be reported to a court or which can be adjusted best without a court being
> drawn in. It is the experience of active children's agencies that for every
> case requiring court intervention, there are four or five that had best not
> go to court at all. [22]

The Third White House Conference organized by the Children's Bureau in 1930, on "child health and protection," also supported this point of view. It was recognized in this conference that since child protection was so largely a preventive social case work job, with less than one-fifth of the cases needing the services of the court, there was no sound basis for placing child protection under the auspices of the juvenile court. It was pointed out that by the time a family whose children are neglected comes to the notice of the juvenile court, it is often too late to rehabilitate it. Protection of children from cruelty and neglect should, therefore, be the responsibility of public or private agencies whose personnel is suitably trained in social work and law.

Although from the beginning, the protective movement had a quasi-public status, in that the agencies were given special statutory powers and privileges to assist in the enforcement of laws relating to the protection of children and punishment of adults, by 1915 leaders in the field were expressing the need for the state to take more responsibility for this program.

> Private societies were necessary in the early development of child protection when the work was experimental, the cases occurring were individual and their application and elasticity and adaptivity were required of the organization involved. In so far as any work becomes based on well established principles, requires more permanent care and involves an element of compulsion or control, it becomes possible for public departments to administer it. [23]

In 1920, Mr. C. C. Carstens in one of his papers presented at the National Conference of Social Work pointed out that:

> There is a principle in human welfare, than which there is none older, namely, that it is the function of the state to provide for the protection if its citizens. This certain applies in the field of child protection. Private societies may initiate and may carry on for many years their special method for arousing the communities interest for the development of standards, but a state cannot be considered well equipped until it has a department of child protection . . . an alert agency in the development of a better world for its children. [24]

The White House Conference of 1930, on child health and protection, emphasized that children's protective work is fundamentally a public responsibility and especially so in situations where clear cut interference with family relations is necessary. [25] Even so, public agencies for child protection were slow in developing.

This conference was an important landmark in the history of child protection for other reasons as well. One of the four committees formulated as a result of this conference published its findings under the title, Dependent and Neglected Children. In the section of this report which dealt with the question of child protection it was pointed out that ignorance, disease, crime, feeble-mindedness, and brutality of various kinds are the contributory factors in child abuse and neglect. As long as these factors exist, children will suffer and there will be need for their protection from some source.

This committee was also instrumental in bringing together for discussions the diverse philosophies which existed in the protective program. By doing so, it was able to clarify not only the points of diversity, but put together some basic assumptions. This was very important and meaningful to everyone interested in the field, since it was the outcome of a national conference which had pooled together all available knowledge, experience, and expert opinion. For the first time, also, a national organization clarified and defined the functions of child protective agencies. It said:

> Child protection is a specialized service in the field of child welfare on behalf of children suffering from cruelty or abuse or whose physical, mental or moral welfare is endangered through the neglect of their parents or custodians, or whose rights or welfare are violated or threatened, . . . Child protection is a distinct form of social service to children. It attacks the various problems of serious child neglect and abuse from the standpoint of parental responsibility for care and protection. It aims to obtain results through advise, persuasion and parental education; but, when necessary to take extreme measures, the agencies are equipped for the effective use of compulsion discipline or punishment through a personnel trained in the use of the law and legal machinery for a social purpose. It is a function of child protection to work for the diminution and improvement of bad community conditions adversely affecting child and family life. Through improvement of community conditions, it seeks the establishment of wholesome standards of family life and the protection of childhood.

> The child protective agency stands as the friend, protector and sometimes the avenger of helpless, oppressed children, the innocent victims of brutality and crime, or vicious and degrading surroundings and of abuse and neglect of every kind.[26]

This was the first general definition of protective work which received wide, though not universal, acceptance. Before this, protective work was defined by various agencies in the field, each giving its own interpretation. The conference must be given credit for clarifying, for agencies engaged in protective work and for others directly and indirectly connected with it, the goals of the service and the method by which these goals could best be achieved.

In this report the committee classified the problems of child protection in two groups.

1.   The individual child and his family. -- This included protection of children from physical cruelty, physical neglect, medical neglect, moral neglect, desertion, non-support and abandonment, neglect of care needed because of defect in mind or body, protection from exploitation, violation of chastity, protection needed by children of illegitimate birth.

2.   Community conditions. -- This involved the removing or improving of community conditions which contribute to the neglect or exploitation of children.[27]

The importance of a wholesome family life for children was greatly stressed by the committee. It was emphasized that nothing else can contribute more to the happiness and well-being of children. Preservation of home for the child should therefore become the basis of protective services.

The best and proper place for a normal child is with his own parents in his own home if that is or can be made a decent home. When conditions are found to be such as to make removal necessary, removal should be temporary with social case work directed toward rehavilitation of the family and restoration of the home. Permanent removal should be the last resort as it is the most serious step.[28]

The Juvenile Protective Associations, a new type of protective agency, had also started developing by the end of the second decade. These agencies were the modern outgrowth of the children's protective movement and in some cases they had formerly been societies for the prevention of cruelty to children. In the beginning they were concerned with the discovery and correction of community conditions that make for juvenile delinquency. However, they also prosecuted in cases of children who had been abused or neglected, and protected unmarried mothers and their children from cruelty and exploitation.[29]

Girls Protective Societies had developed in many places. These societies, in addition to helping girls who were in moral difficulties or had become unmarried mothers, also rendered valuable child protective services.[30]

The importance of the police role in the protective aspects of children's programs was being recognized and the report on dependent and neglected children stated:

> The employment of policewomen is rapidly gaining in favor throughout the country and over one hundred and fifty cities have already adopted this service. . . . Policewomen are not primarily charged with the protection of life and property and the preservation of peace as are policemen. Rather they are concerned with the legal and social problems of women, girls and children, who come to the attention of the police through crime or delinquency or who are the victims of crime. They are also concerned with the discovery and protection of those who are exposed to danger of the violation of the law, especially its moral code, serving them along preventive social case work lines and calling on the communities' social agencies for specialized services as needed.[31]

Another milestone in the field during the third decade was the starting of the social security programs. The Social Security Act of 1935 provided financial aid to the states, through the Children's Bureau, for establishing and strengthening both in the urban and rural areas, services for the protection and care of homeless, dependent and neglected children. The depression made it necessary for the federal government, and through it the state and local governments. to assume responsibility for child welfare and other social welfare services to an unprecedented degree.

While, on one hand, protective work was being accepted more and more as a public responsibility and various types of child welfare agencies were adding this program to their existing one, progressive child welfare agencies were attempting the application of casework method in the field. This was possible because trained social workers were available and protective work was being accepted more as a preventive and rehabilitative program, requiring trained workers.

Child protection is a difficult specialty in the child welfare field. Successful work with parents who are indifferent, stubborn, often vicious and resentful of interference, requires workers educated, trained and skilled for the work. . . . These processes, social investigation, social diagnosis, and social treatment, constitute social case work. Clearly child protection is a form of social case work.[32]

In spite of this recognition, trained workers were reluctant to get into protective work, and the application of case work method in the field had many obstacles. This was so because authority is fundamental in protective service and for several years after case work had developed and was accepted as a method of helping individuals in need, there were many misconceptions about the use of authority, which was looked upon as a word synonymous with harshness. Social workers struggled with the problem of approaching a parent with a complaint of neglect, showing him that the community disapproves of what he has been failing to do for his child, holding him to the need to bring about change and, at the same time, giving him the due respect as a person and as a parent. Case work had long accepted the premise that before the case work process can begin, the client must be aware of his need and seek help. But in the case of a neglecting parent where the complaint often comes from the community, there seems a denial of this concept.

However, it was gradually recognized that authority is also a responsible use of professional knowledge; every social agency must act with some authority and must assume authority in deciding whether to give the requested help, in defining what must be expected of the client and what he can expect from the agency. A protective agency uses its authority in the interests of helping the parents as well as the children. The community gives the agency the right to inquire into whether and how children are being harmed and to help the parents discover what they can do to provide their children with the care they need, and to offer help to realize the desired objectives.[33]

Since the starting in 1935 of federal aid to states for developing child welfare programs, public child welfare agencies have developed very rapidly over all the country. These services with the goal of providing protection and care to dependent and neglected children in their own homes, are supposed to encompass child protective services too. However, if one looks closely at the picture, the child protection program shows an uneven development in the past and offers considerable evidence of the existence of a confused state of affairs even today.

There seems to be no uniform approach to this problem and no universal definition of the scope and nature of this specialized service. This is reflected in the report of the nationwide survey made recently by the Children's Division of the American Humane Association, Denver, Colorado.[34] This report gives facts and figures about the number of public and private agencies in each state, specifically offering protective services to children. At the time of the survey, thirty-two states and the District of Columbia had no private agency with child protective function and fifteen states reported no legislative or legal provision in the state law, imposing responsibility for child protective services on the public agency.

Protection of Neglected and Abused Children
in Los Angeles[35]

The responsibility of protecting the neglected and abused children in Los Angeles was first shouldered by the present Los Angeles Children's Bureau, earlier known as the Juvenile Protective Association. This association was the outcome of a juvenile court committee, established in 1903, to strengthen the work of the juvenile court. The committee was originally responsible for organizing and providing voluntary probation officers but later became the Juvenile Improvement Association and secured the enactment of child labor laws and other protective legislation for children. In 1912 the association was reincorporated as the Juvenile Protective Association and aimed at eradicating conditions in the community believed to be harmful to children, as well as handling a small number of neglect and abuse cases. Until 1920, this association was the only organization handling child protective work in the county and, until the establishment of the Los Angeles Community Chest in 1924, was financed by membership fees, donations, benefits, and in small part by the County Board of Supervisors. By 1928 the association became the Children's Protective Association and extended its activities to preventive work in the field of juvenile delinquency, rehabilitation of broken homes, and placement of children away from home if necessary.

The depression of 1930 resulted in the creation of many new welfare agencies, some of which accepted some responsibility for children. By 1935 the Family Welfare Association began to accept cases of child neglect in established homes, Jewish and Catholic welfare agencies accepted some responsibility for children of their faith, and the Crime Prevention Bureau of the Police Department gradually assumed responsibility for cases of extreme cruelty which were formerly handled by the Children's Protective Association. After 1937 the association was aiding unmarried mothers and accepting applications for foster care for children. In 1940 the association was renamed the Los Angeles Children's Bureau and during the following decade greatly expanded its foster care and adoption program in response to the needs of the community during the war and post-war years. In its present set-up it is no longer a protective agency.

The increase in population after the war necessitated an increase in both private and public welfare activities and the need for a clear-cut protective program received legal recognition in Part 4 of Division 2 of the Welfare and Institutions Code, which made provision for such a program.[36]

In April 1957, the Board of Supervisors authorized the Bureau of Public Assistance to establish a pilot study in protective services in Los Angeles. To make this possible, the board authorized funds in the amount of $32,000.00 per year to finance this study. This study was expected to last approximately three to four years before being finally evaluated.[37] It is presently being carried on by the Protective Unit of the Division of Child Welfare Services of the Bureau of Public Assistance in an area bounded on the north by Griffith Park and the Los Angeles River, on the east by Lucas and Douglas Streets and Elysian Park, on the south by Seventh Street, and on the west by Vermont Avenue.[38]

Services in this project are not restricted to those families receiving relief.

Other families receiving services are those in which the parental function needs assistance because it is either causing harm to children or requires assistance over a period of time. Families which include a child under ten years of age are given priority.

So far, referrals have come mostly from interested individuals, schools, and a variety of social agencies. Medical social workers have made requests for service and there have been a few police requests. It is hoped that the study will help to determine the extent of the need for protective service in Los Angeles and throw some light on how such services can best be given.

Footnotes

[1] Grace Abbott, The Child and the State (Chicago: The University of Chicago Press, 1938), Vol. I, p. 3.

[2] Chester G. Verniger, Parent and Child (Stanford: Stanford University Press, 1936), p. 17.

[3] E. E. Bowerman, The Laws of Child Protection, (London: Sir Isaac Pitman and Sons Ltd., 1933), p. 8.

[4] Ibid., pp. 8-9.

[5] Abbott, op.cit., p. 7.

[6] Homer Folks, The Care of Destitute, Neglected and Delinquent Children (New York: The Macmillan Co., 1911), pp. 168-69.

[7] Ibid., p. 11.

[8] Abbott, op.cit., pp. 59-60.

[9] Forty-Seventh Annual Report of the American Humane Association, 1923 (Boston: American Humane Society, 1924), p. 4.

[10] William J. Shultz, The Humane Movement in the United States, 1910-1922 (New York: Columbia University Press, 1924), p. 11.

[11] Roswell C. McCrea, The Humane Movement (New York: Columbia University Press, 1910), p. 135.

[12] Ibid., pp. 135-36.

[13] Ibid., p. 137.

[14]Ibid., p. 141.

[15]Ibid., pp. 142-143.

[16]Ibid., pp. 145-146.

[17]Emma O. Lundberg, Unto the Least of These (New York: D. Appleton-Century Company, 1947), p. 114

[18]Ibid., p. 113.

[19]Ibid., p. 124.

[20]C. C. Carstens, "The Development of Social Work for Child Protection," The Annals of the American Academy of Political and Social Sciences, Vol. XCVIII (November 1921), p. 135.

[21]Ibid., p. 138.

[22]C. C. Carstens, "The Next Steps in the Work of Child Protection," Proceedings of the National Conference of Social Work, 1924 (Chicago: Univ. of Chicago Press), p. 136.

[23]Schultz, op.cit., pp. 223-224.

[24]C. C. Carstens, "A Community Program in the Care of Neglected Children," Proceedings of the National Conference of Social Work, 1920, p. 139.

[25]Dependent and Neglected Children, White House Conference on Child Health and Protection, 1933, Section IV (New York: Appleton-Century Company), p. 372.

[26]Ibid., pp. 354-355.

[27]Ibid., pp. 355-359.

[28]Ibid., pp. 364-365.

[29]Ray S. Hubbard, "Child Protection," Social Work Yearbook, 1929 (New York: Russell Sage Foundation), p. 66.

[30]Dependent and Neglected Children, p. 374.

[31]Ibid., p. 374.

[32]Ibid., p. 360.

[33]Henrietta L. Gordon, "Criminal Neglect of Children--Who Is Guilty?" Child Welfare, February 1953, p. 10.

[34]Vincent DeFrancis, Child Protection Services in the United States (Denver: The American Humane Association, 1956), pp. 36-41.

[35]For an excellent detailed account of this program, the reader is referred to Dorothy Frances Allen, "The Changing Emphasis in Protective Services to Children" (unpublished Master's thesis, University of Southern California, 1943).

[36]State of California, Welfare and Institutions Code, p. 144.

[37]The final evaluation of the study is expected in July 1961.

[38]While some parts of this geographic area are the same as covered by the Central Division of the Juvenile Police Department, at the time of this study the Protective Unit had just come into existence.

CHAPTER III

DEVELOPMENT OF THE JUVENILE POLICE SYSTEM

This chapter discusses briefly the development and function of the police, the women police, and the juvenile police in the United States. The Juvenile Division of the Los Angeles Police is discussed at the end of the chapter.

Development of the Police System

[The police power] is an inherent power of government which gives the social group as a whole the right to make and enforce rules for general welfare and safety on its individual members. It is to be found in every organized social body whether simple and primitive or complex and civilized. It means social control and it is as essential to group preservation against attack from within as is the power to make war on threatening groups from without.[1]

In every society today, government maintains the internal law and order by exercising this power through its police force. The police are thus the chief agents of law enforcement, which often entails apprehension and arrest of offenders. The functions of police, even within the limits of law enforcement, are broad, and are interpreted differently in different parts of the world under different forms of government.

The beginnings of our police procedure today are to be found in Anglo-Saxon England, when the peace was maintained by means of a "frank pledge" in which all citizens were responsible for the good behavior of others in the same group. This has significance today in the fact that all citizens share certain powers of arrest.[2]

Long before the "frank pledge" system came into use there were other systems, purely Anglo-Saxon in origin, which were in use.[3] The city police system in England can be traced back to the time of Edward I, when a "watch and ward" was first set up to maintain peace in the city. However, as the population increased, this system proved ineffective and finally a metropolitan police system was established in 1829 by Sir Robert Peel.

In the United States of America, the colonies followed the plan of the English police system to a very great extent. Some of the basic ideas and procedures were adopted and developed with the passage of time. At first, only a system of "night watch" was established in New England, which was followed by a system of "watch and ward" in Philadelphia, where all citizens took turns to perform the duty. "According to the rules, watchmen were required to walk their rounds slowly and silently and now and then stand still and listen and cry the time of the night and state of the weather."[4] At first, these night watchmen were all volunteers. Gradually, they became paid watchmen who did other work during the day.

However, as the population increased so did the problems, and the night watchman system proved ineffective. Many watchmen could not keep awake at night because they were working during the day as well, and this system offered no protection at all to the community during the day. Hence the idea of organizing day forces developed. Boston was the first city in the United States to appoint a group of men for day watch (six men in 1838). Soon, New York and Philadelphia followed the example. But the separation of day and night forces caused friction and inefficiency, especially in an atmosphere of disorder and race riots. The New York legislature, therefore, in 1844, created a police force of 800 men with a chief of police for New York State. This police force was a united day and night force and was similar to the force in London. It formed the basis for developing a modern urban police organization in the United States.[5]

Police Systems in the United States

The police forces in the United States operate at four main levels[6] which may be described as local, county, state, and federal. Since child protection laws derive their authority from the separate states, it is evident that only those police whose jurisdiction falls within the borders of a state will normally be responsible for the child protection.

Local Police

Every village, town, and city has a police force which may range in size from the lone, unpaid, untrained marshal to the highly complex, efficient force of several thousand men such as the Los Angeles City Police Department. The local police are directly responsible for the protection of the children in their community, and large communities such as Los Angeles have found it necessary to establish a special police division for juveniles.

County Police

Each state is divided into counties and every county has an elected sheriff. During the days following the western expansion the sheriff was the main local law enforcement agent, but the progress of civilization has brought about the collapse of the sheriff system in the vast majority of American counties and has made the sheriff largely an anachronism.[7]

There are, however, some remarkable exceptions where the sheriff and his deputies have evolved into an important modern police force.

More ambitious is the scheme developed and put into effect in the Los Angeles County, California. . . . In its formal aspects, this force is one of the most highly developed county police agencies to be found in the United States.[8]

The sheriff is responsible for law enforcement and hence child protection within his county where the local police force is ineffective or nonexistent.

State Police

The inability of state governments to secure statewide observance of state laws because of areas of weak, local law enforcement has been responsible for the growth of state police forces. In general, child neglect or abuse comes to the attention of local or county police. There are, however, cases of child abduction or traveling parents and cases in remote locations which state police are better able to detect or intercept.

Federal Police

Federal law enforcement agencies are not responsible for enforcing state laws for child protection. Nevertheless, they do have responsibility for enforcing federal statutes.

Development of Women Police

In the United States it was not until the emphasis in the field of child welfare shifted from punishment to prevention and from prevention to vital welfare that the need for special police to work with juveniles was felt. With the passing of the first juvenile court law by the Illinois legislature in 1899, and the establishment of the first juvenile court in July of the same year, a positive interest in the welfare of the delinquent, neglected, dependent, and abused children was established. The early juvenile protective associations in the various large cities worked closely with the juvenile courts and police and helped to investigate the family background and circumstances of the youngsters brought before the juvenile courts. However, before recruiting men police for this work, women police were given this responsibility.

The need for a different approach in relation to children and youth led to a specialization in this aspect of police work. In 1905 at Portland, Oregon, the first policewoman was assigned to preventive protective work with girls.[10] Before this period women police had existed, but were mainly assigned duties in women's jails and with women prisoners.

The beginning of socialization of police work lay in the appointment of matrons in 1888 and 1889, who were to look after the physical needs of the women's quarters in jails, workhouse, police stations and of the women and children held therein. Later they served also as escorts for insane women committed to hospitals and for girls and women taken to court. [11]

The policewomen's movement which, as stated earlier, began in Oregon in 1905, had a rapid development and reached New York in 1908. In 1909 the Juvenile Bureau of the Los Angeles Police was initiated. [12] In the following six years, twenty states had appointed women police to handle the cases of women and children. [13] While this idea was accepted readily and many states appointed women police, their duties and responsibilities were not standardized; police departments in different states used their services in different ways. In some states, for example, they were assigned the duties of probation officers. Some other states assigned them the domestic relations cases; their main duty here was to see that deserting husbands paid weekly alimony to their wives.

In general it was true that the nature of the work of policewomen depended upon the initiative of the individual worker and upon her ability to interpret the work to the police authorities. [14]

> The work of policewomen in different towns and cities has also been found to differ according to the number and character of social agencies in these communities. For example in cities where there are strong juvenile protective associations or societies for the prevention of cruelty to children, these associations have been doing much of the work outlined by another city as the duty of policewomen . . . . Although progress in standardizing the work of the policewomen has been very slow and officials in different cities have conceived of the work quite differently, the real purpose has not been lost sight of and women with police powers are seeing more and more clearly that their greatest task and opportunity lie in the field of protective work. [15]

During the 1920's there was a keen awareness about the training of policewomen, especially those who were directors or heads of the women's bureau. Trained social workers were preferred for these positions, because it was felt that the job required not only knowledge of laws and police rules and regulations but also the knowledge and ability to deal with human beings with insight and understanding. In 1924, Van Winkle wrote:

> Social workers did not enter this field until very recently, but the movement for their appointment gained impetus during the war when trained social workers were employed to put into practice preventive measures for the benefit of men in the Army and Navy and for girls and women camp followers . . . . We must therefore train policewomen in special schools. For this purpose two years ago, the Boston School of Public Service was established. Last year George Washington University offered a training course and the New York School of Social Work trained qualified social workers for positions as police executives. [16]

Police work of women was viewed as social work, and it was felt that unless police services and social services of a community were integrated, the delinquent children would be passed from one agency to another. Socialized police work was considered an extension of the government's responsibility for public welfare. [17]

Development of Juvenile Police

While these developments were taking place in recruiting and training women police, the police departments in large cities where juvenile delinquency was on the increase were becoming more and more aware of the fact that juvenile offenders required a special approach by all police, men and women, who came in contact with them. By 1914 the New York City Police had made organized and conscious effort to avoid indiscriminate arrests and to help the youthful offenders, wherever possible, through "admonition and warning." They launched what was felt to be a preventive program. Their activities included protecting children from the influence of bad gangs; locating mental defectives among arrested youths; making friends of those groups who had long been enemies of the police by relieving their distress and destitution. [18]

The Junior Police program was set up about the same time, with its aim to establish better relations between police and children. To encourage this, police organized athletics and military drills, emphasized citizenship and good conduct, and visited schools to deliver safety lectures to pupils. After a few years, this program was taken up by the educational system.

During 1915 and 1916, another program was started in New York. Young police officers were introduced to "preventive and protective views" in police work. The older and more experienced officers who were given the responsibility of training the younger ones were known as "welfare lieutenants." Among their duties was the protection of young people. As the program developed, the welfare lieutenants observed parks and other premises closely, cooperated with the board of education in truancy cases, investigated cases of destitution which had resulted in neglect of children or in delinquency. The development of Crime Prevention Bureaus in the 1920's[19] and the Juvenile Aid Bureau in the 1930's[20] in New York and other states is an example of the efforts made by the police during that period in helping the delinquent, neglected, abused, and dependent children.

Studies of adult criminals in the late 1920's had emphasized the fact that the anti-social careers of criminals started and could be detected early in life. At the same time, communities in the fast growing industrial areas were becoming concerned about the large number of young offenders who were appearing before the courts every day. The Crime Prevention Bureaus were the outcome of the communities' concern to prevent juvenile delinquency. Alfred J. Kahn, discussing the focus of the New York City's Crime Prevention Bureau, states, "As the Bureau defined its focus, it formulated a two-fold prevention program: (1) the controlling of contributing community conditions and (2) the treatment of potential delinquents."[21]

Crime Prevention Bureaus in other states developed with similar objectives. However, since 1905, when the first policewoman was appointed in Portland, Oregon, a large number of police departments in many cities with populations over 25,000 have established separate units or appointed a specialist for work with children. The growth of these units has been rapid and, unfortunately, somewhat haphazard.[22] Each state has developed them to meet its need in its own way.

Juvenile Police Department of the City of Los Angeles

The Juvenile Division of Police in Los Angeles City was established in 1909 as the Juvenile Bureau with the appointment of Mrs. Alice Wells as the first policewomen; the following year the position was put under civil service.[23] A few years later, Mrs. Wells, discussing the policewomen in Los Angeles, said:

> In asking the city officials of Los Angeles to create a position for me as a regular police officer, an integral and permanent part of the department, so that the protective and preventive side for women and children might be developed within the department, I based the petition upon the plea that dance halls, skating rinks, picture shows, and the streets including the curfew law could not properly be cared for by men officers.[24]

In the report of the Los Angeles Police Department for the year 1911-1912 it was noted that the policewomen investigated cases of children referred to the Juvenile Bureau, located lost persons, and protected young girls from bad associates in public halls and motion picture theatres.[25] As it grew and developed with the growth of the city, it worked closely with the Crime Prevention Bureau of the Police Department which handled cases of delinquency, neglect, and extreme cruelty to children requiring immediate court action.

In its present set-up, the Juvenile Division is a part of the Patrol Bureau of Police.[26] For the purpose of effective operation, police have divided the city into fourteen geographic divisions;[27] each division has a juvenile unit. These units are responsible for controlling and preventing anti-social activities of juveniles and minors in the city. They are also responsible for protecting juveniles and minors who are victims of adult neglect, cruelty, and abuse. The headquarters of the Juvenile Division, which is at Georgia Street, is open twenty-four hours every day. The other juvenile units are open between 8:00 A.M. and 1:00 A.M. However, in emergency cases, juvenile police services are made available through the juvenile headquarters, to any part of the city, between the hours of 1:00 A.M. and 8:00 A.M.

At the time of this study (June 1959) there was a total of 211 juvenile police officers in the fourteen divisions, covering an area of 433 square miles in the city.

Men officers for juvenile work are selected from among the trained police officers already in service with the police department. There is no recruitment to the Juvenile Division of any male officer who has not had three or four years of experience (preferably four years) in other areas of law enforcement. This police is to insure that officers working with juvenile cases have the ability and skill to work with children who need help.

During the initial twelve weeks training period of the police officers at the police academy, all trainees are given theoretical and practical training in all areas of law enforcement and related fields. One of these is "Juvenile Police and Procedure," which covers laws pertaining to Juveniles in the Welfare and Institutions Code and the Penal Code of the State of California. A background of juvenile work and the organization and functions of the Juvenile Division are discussed. Lectures are given on causes of juvenile delinquency, juvenile detention and arrest policy, adult cases involving juveniles, and the juvenile police patrol function.

A male police officer who has been in service with the department for three or four years and is interested in juvenile work may make an application to the Juvenile Division. However, he is selected only if the appointing officer, after interviewing him and screening reports from the various supervisors under whom he has worked, is convinced that he has the necessary qualities and skill for working with children. Not all police officers who apply for juvenile work are selected; neither do those who are selected remain in the division unless they are found suitable for carrying on the work entrusted to them.

Women police are often sent directly to work in the Juvenile Division after their initial training of four weeks. This is so because services of women police are utilized mainly in the Women's Section of the jail and in the Juvenile Division of the Police Department. As fresh recruits in the Juvenile Division, they work with and under the supervision of an experienced officer; their services in the division are essential because law requires that girls between the ages of five and seventeen years should be dealt with, whenever possible, by a policewoman.

A few senior men and women police officers in the Juvenile Division are selected from time to time to attend a course at the Delinquency Control Institute of the University of Southern California. This institute offers three-month courses twice every year to police officers, probation officers, and others who work with juveniles. The objective of the training is to impart a better understanding of the social and legal aspects of the causes, prevention, and control of problems relating to juveniles.

All juvenile police in Los Angeles City work in plain clothes and use unmarked cars when they go out on official duty. The night patrol officers cruise in the cars in their geographic district between 4:30 P.M. and 1:15 A.M. For reasons of efficiency and safety, night patrol officers go out in pairs, preferably a man and a woman. The cars they use are installed with a two-way radio. This makes it possible for them to attend to complaints which come to the headquarters while they are cruising. When not attending to any specific calls, the patrolling officers cruise near bus depots, parks, coffee shops, and other places where they know from experience they might find juveniles either causing trouble or being troubled and needing help. For example, some coffee shops in the Los Angeles area are known to be places frequented by prostitutes, drunks, and homosexuals. Patrolling officers in that area drive by these coffee shops at least two or three times during an evening to see if any juveniles are in need of protection. If they see them, they talk to them and find out where they live and why they are there. They are counseled and if necessary their parents are contacted; this is one of the protective functions of the juvenile police.

While the night patrol officers attend to the complaints of juvenile delinquency, neglect, cruelty, and abuse which are received between the hours of 4:30 P.M. and 1:15 A.M. and take action which is immediately necessary, detailed investigation of cases is done by the staff on duty during the day. This is done not only because the night staff is very limited in number but also because it is possible to contact the neighbors, relatives, schools, and other agencies during the day for obtaining the necessary facts on a case.

The method of investigation of the juvenile police and their step-by-step activities in working with cases of child neglect and abuse are discussed in Chapters IV and V, respectively.

Footnotes

[1] Helen D. Pigeon and others, Principles and Methods in Dealing with Offenders (Philadelphia: Pennsylvania Valley Publishers, Inc., 1949), p. 5.

[2] Ibid., p. 7.

[3] (a) bohr: meaning surety or suretyship; (b) gegildan: meaning community of gild brotheren, association of freeman or gilds who assumed responsibility of kin, when they were unable to do so themselves; (c) tything: inhabitants were organized in groups of ten, with one leader responsible for the discharge by the nine others of the duties prescribed for them. Ten such groups were organized as a "hynden" or hundred under one headman who directed the ten leaders.

[4] Pigeon, op. cit., p. 8.

[5] Ibid., p. 8.

[6] Charles Reith, The Blind Eye of History (London: Faber and Faber, Ltd., 1952), p. 97.

[7] Bruce Smith, Police Systems in the United States (New York: Harper and Brothers Publishers, 1949), p. 89.

[8] Ibid., p. 106.

[10] Lynn D. Swanson, "Police and Children," The Police Chief, June 1958, p. 22.

[11] Mina Van Winkle, "The Policewoman," Proceedings of the National Conference of Social Work (Chicago: The University of Chicago Press, 1924), p. 187.

[12] Swanson, op, cit., p. 22.

[13] Alice Wells, "The Policewoman's Movement--Present Status and Future Needs," Proceedings of the National Conference of Charities and Corrections (Chicago: The

Hildmann Printing Co., 1916), p. 547.

[14]Mina Van Winkle, "Standardization of Aims and Methods of Work of Policewomen," Proceeding of the National Conference of Social Work (Chicago: Rogers and Hall, 1919), p. 135.

[15]Ibid., pp. 135-136.

[16]Van Winkle, "The Policewomen," op. cit., p. 188.

[17]Ibid., p. 192.

[18]Alfred J. Kahn, Police and Children, A Study of New York City's Juvenile Aid Bureau (New York: Citizen's Committee on Children of New York City, Inc., 1951), p. 12.

[19]Ibid., pp. 12-13.

[20]Ibid., p. 14.

[21]Ibid., p. 13.

[22]Swanson, op.cit., p. 22.

[23]Van Winkle, "Standardization of Aims and Methods of Work of Policewomen," op.cit., p. 134.

[24]Alice Wells, "Policewomen of Los Angeles, California," Proceedings of the National Conference of Charities and Corrections (Chicago: The Hildmann Printing Co., 1915), p. 412.

[25]Van Winkle, "Standardization of Aims and Methods of Work of Policewomen," op.cit., p. 135.

[26]The other six bureaus are Personnel and Training Bureau, Technical Services Bureau, Bureau of Administration, Traffic Bureau, Detective Bureau, and the Bureau of Corrections.

[27]Since the time of this study the number of geographic divisions has increased to fifteen.

CHAPTER IV

ANALYSIS OF CASES OF NEGLECT

This chapter contains an analysis of 70 cases selected from a total of 137 cases of child neglect which were investigated by the juvenile police of the Central Division of the City of Los Angeles during the year of 1958. A preliminary study of all 137 cases was made but only those completed cases for which the officers responsible were readily available could be selected for detailed analysis. The 70 cases selected therefore represent approximately a 50 percent sample of the total. This is not a random sample, it is a 100 percent sample of all cases for which the officers responsible were readily available for interview.

The analysis comprises a classification of the cases within several different categories and a discussion of the juvenile police action from initial contact to final disposition.

The cases are first classified according to the nature of the neglect and the particular sections of the Welfare and Institutions Code or the Penal Code under which the juvenile police have taken action. Further classification of the cases is presented under various sub-headings in a section containing factual information about the families and the source and method of complaint of neglect as received by the juvenile police. The activities of the juvenile police are discussed under the general headings of investigation procedures and decision making.

Neglect Defined

Webster's New International Dictionary defines the word "neglect" as "lack of diligence or care; omission of duty."[1] Black's Law Dictionary defines it to mean "omit, fail or forebear to do a thing that can be done; unwillingness to perform one's duty."[2]

The doctrine of negligence is stated by Black's Law Dictionary "to rest on duty of every person to exercise due care in his conduct toward others from which injury may result."[3] The term "negligence" is defined as "omission to do something which a reasonable man, guided by those ordinary considerations which ordinarily regulate human affairs would do or the doing of something which a reasonable or prudent man would not do."[4] The term "neglected minor" is defined as "one suffering from neglect and in a state of want."[5] Within the legal frame of reference, inaction as well as action may be negligence. It is immaterial to the question of negligence whether the violated standard of conduct is established by statute or by the common law.

Legislation to protect minors from adult neglect and abuse is to be found in the statutes of every state in the United States. Though these laws differ from one state to another, there is universal acceptance in all the states of the principle of the right of one child to protection from neglect and abuse.[6] In the State of California, laws protecting the neglected, dependent, and abused children are incorporated both in the Welfare and Institutions Code as well as the Penal Code. Sections of these codes appropriate to the present study are to be found in Appendix A.

Types of Charge

The 70 cases of neglect selected for this study are classified in Table 1 according to the type of charge under which they were booked[7] by juvenile police.

TABLE 1

DISTRIBUTION OF NEGLECT CASES ACCORDING TO THE TYPE OF CHARGE

Type of Charge	Number of Cases
Section 700b of the Welfare and Institutions Code	32
Section 700d of the Welfare and Institutions Code	23
Section 273a of the Penal Code	15
Total	70

While the various sections and subsections of the two codes make provisions for protecting the minor from different types of dependency and neglect situations, as indicated in Table 1, the bulk of the dependency and neglect cases in this study were booked under Section 700b and Section 700d of the Welfare and Institutions Code of California.

Section 700b applies to juveniles (i.e., persons under the age of 18 years) who have either no parents or guardians or whose parents and guardians are not willing or able to exercise proper parental supervision and control.

Section 700d applies to all minors (i.e., persons under the age of 21 years) whose home is an unfit place by reason of neglect, cruelty, or depravity on the part of parents or guardians or any other adult responsible for their custody or care. Cases booked under Section 700b may also come under Section 700d though in such cases both allegations may be included in one.

Section 273a of the Penal Code of California applies to any person who wilfully causes or inflicts unjustifiable pain or mental suffering on a child or causes or permits the life and limb of a child to be in danger or the health of a child to be injured. Such a person is guilty of a misdemeanor. [8]

These three statutes cover most kinds of dependency, neglect, physically unfit, and morally and emotionally unfit situations to which a child may be exposed by his parents or guardian.

Cases Booked Under Section 700b of the Welfare and Institutions Code

In this study, the 32 cases booked under Section 700b of the Welfare and Institutions Code frequently were situations where one or both parents left their children without adult supervision while they were out for long or short periods of time, either for work or pleasure. The following examples from the study illustrate such situations.

Illustration I (Neglect Case)

A neighbor telephoned the juvenile police at 10 P.M. one night and informed them that two young boys, eight and ten years of age, were being left alone by the mother for long periods of time, during the day and night. When police went to investigate at 11 P.M. they found the two boys in bed, but without an adult in the house. They questioned the boys about their mother's whereabouts and were told that she had gone out with a boy friend at about 8 P.M. after giving them supper. Upon further questioning, they said that she often went out in the evenings after giving them supper and sometimes was out all night. There was enough food in the house and things were well organized. Police observed that the boys seemed mature and capable of looking after themselves and looked well taken care of. The house also was well kept and neat.

In this case, while the physical neglect was of a minor nature and the boys, at least outwardly, seemed to be able to take care of themselves, the woman showed signs of failing in her role as a mother by being away for long periods and also sometimes leaving her sons overnight without any adult care. The juvenile police officers, after making the necessary investigation, decided that the neglect situation did not warrant removal of the children to Juvenile Hall. They left a note for the mother to contact them at the Juvenile Police Division the following morning.

Certain types of dependency cases are also booked under this section. In these cases one or both parents are physically or mentally ill and unable to care for their children. The following examples illustrate these situations.

Illustration II (Dependency Due to Mental Ill Health)

The Los Angeles General Hospital telephoned the Juvenile Police and informed them that Mrs. B. had voluntarily committed herself to the Psychiatric Unit of the Los Angeles General Hospital that day. She had told them that her little daughter, two years of age, was at her home and that she did not want her daughter to be taken care of by any relatives. Mrs. B. was in her late twenties. Her husband's whereabouts were not known. She had no stable source of income as she was not able to keep a job for any length of time. She felt depressed and unable to care for herself and her child.

Juvenile police officers went to Mrs. B's home, took custody of the child and removed her to the Lathrop Section of Juvenile Hall. [9]

Illustration III (Dependency Due to Physical Ill Health)

Mrs. C. had to be admitted to the hospital for the birth of her second baby and for possible surgery. She left her 18 month old daughter in the care of her neighbor. After taking care of the daughter for two days, the neighbor found that she could not continue. She telephoned the police and asked them to make some arrangement for the child, because the mother had no relatives in this city who could care for this little girl.

Cases Booked Under Section 700d of the Welfare and Institutions Code

Illustration IV (Child Exposed to Immoral Living Conditions)

One night a neighbor telephoned the juvenile police and reported that Mr. and Mrs. D. were making a public nuisance of themselves by having a loud and violent quarrel and a child was involved. Police went to the house and found Mr. D. in a very drunk condition. While the parents, who were in their middle thirties, were busy fighting, their nine year old girl was very scared and was trying to hide behind doors and furniture. When she saw the police, she ran to hide herself in the garage.

Neighbors informed the juvenile police that the couple drank and got into fights frequently and the girl witnessed all their quarrels. She was also aware of the fact that her mother was living with a man without being married to him. During these fights the child, who was always very scared, cried, and attempted to hide behind doors or furniture. She often took refuge in the garage or in a neighbor's house.

After questioning the neighbors and the girl, juvenile police were convinced that this was not an isolated incident of drinking and quarreling of the parents in the presence of the child. Their living together in common-law relationship was an added factor to make it an "unfit" home for this girl. The mother was arrested for exposing her child to immoral living conditions and the girl was removed to Juvenile Hall.

Illustration V (Child Neglected and Left Uncared For)

Juvenile police received a call around midnight one evening from a woman (who was not willing to identify herself) about a little girl who was left alone in an apartment. Upon reaching the given address, police found a two year old girl all alone. Neighbors informed the juvenile police officers that the mother had been arrested that day for prostitution. Her common-law husband had disappeared from the house after the woman was arrested, leaving the child alone. Mrs. E. was a Caucasian and her common-law husband was Negro. He was the father of this girl.

Police could not question the child as she was too young. Neighbors and relatives when questioned said that the mother was not a suitable person to care for this child. She drank and indulged in prostitution. Police took custody of the child, removed her to Juvenile Hall, and filed a petition[10] for a suitable foster home placement for her, as the mother was not a fit person to care for her or to provide a normal home for the child.

Cases of extreme neglect where the life and limb of children or their health are endangered because of parental neglect are booked under 273a of the Penal Code. Out of the 70 cases analyzed for this study, 15 were booked under this section. While this is not an indication of the possible percentage of such cases in the city, it does indicate (and was also substantiated by officers interviewed) that severe neglect situations of this kind are comparatively less frequent than those that are classed under Section 700b and 700d of the Welfare and Institutions Code. The following examples illustrate such cases.

Cases Booked Under Section 273a of the Penal Code

Illustration VI (Severe Neglect Endangering Life and Health of Children)

A neighbor telephoned the juvenile police and complained about four children, all under seven years of age, who had been left alone by their parents, Mr. and Mrs. F., since the previous day. The youngest was only two months old. The juvenile police went to this home and found the children by themselves. Their physical condition was filthy and the house was extremely dirty. There was a strong urine odor in the house and dirty clothes were scattered all around. The kitchen was filthy and full of dirty dishes piled up everywhere. There was no food in the house.

Upon questioning the neighbors, juvenile police found out that the parents, Mr. and Mrs. F., were in their early thirties and lived in common-law relationship. They both drank heavily and often. Mr. F. was serving a jail sentence on drunk charges at this time. Mrs. F. frequently left the children alone for several hours without any adult supervision, when she went out to drink. On this occasion she had been gone for two days. Juvenile police later found out that she had gone to San Bernardino with two men whom she had met in a bar.

The children's maternal grandmother, who lived a few blocks away, was contacted. She came to the house and stated that the neglect situation was a chronic one. She or the neighbors frequently fed the children when they were hungry and the parents were away. The parents had no steady source of income. Mrs. F. was arrested upon her return to the house for violating Section 273a of the Penal Code and the children were admitted to Juvenile Hall the same night. Police filed a petition on behalf of the children for their proper care and supervision.

In this case, the mother's negligence toward her children was of an extreme kind. She left them, including a two month old baby and a year old child, for several hours at a time in a filthy house without any food, endangering their health and lives. The following example illustrates another case of extreme neglect.

Illustration VII (Severe Neglect Endangering Life and Health of Child)

Mr. and Mrs. G., a young couple in their early twenties, were spotted by the traffic police at 6 A.M. on a winter morning, while the couple were driving, supposedly toward home, after being out all night. Both of them were in an extremely intoxicated condition. Their four month old baby girl was sleeping in the back seat of the car with very little clothing and in a dripping wet condition. The temperature at this time was below 50 degrees. Upon questioning they told the police that their child had been left in the car when they went from one bar to another.

Traffic police in this case arrested both parents on drunk charges and for violation of Section 273a of the Penal Code. The juvenile police were contacted, and they placed the infant in Juvenile Hall.

Factual Information About the Neglect Cases

Racial Origin

Racial origin of the 70 cases selected for this study is as follows:

TABLE 2

DISTRIBUTION OF NEGLECT CASES ACCORDING TO RACIAL ORIGIN

Racial Origin	Number of Cases
Caucasians	41
Mexicans	19
Negroes	6
Orientals	2
Indians	2
Total	70

The large number of cases in the Mexican and Caucasian groups is explained by the fact that about 96 percent of the 161,000 total population of the Central District was Caucasian (this included the Mexican group also) and only 4 percent was Negro and others. [11]

Marital Status

In the group of 70 neglect cases under study, three out of five of the cases had only one parent in the family. In the 42 cases with only one parent in the home, this parent was nearly always the mother, who was more often deserted or divorced than widowed. The following table gives the details.

TABLE 3

DISTRIBUTION OF NEGLECT CASES ACCORDING TO MARITAL STATUS OF PARENTS

Living with	Number of Families	One Parent		
		Deceased	Divorced	Deserted
Both parents	28	--	--	--
Mother only	39	4	13	22
Father only	3	1	--	2
Total	70			

Age and Sex of Children

The number of neglected children in the 70 families was 137, out of which 60 percent were boys and 40 percent girls. Their distribution according to age is shown by Table 4.

TABLE 4

DISTRIBUTION OF NEGLECTED CHILDREN ACCORDING TO SEX AND AGE

Age Group	Boys	Girls	Total
Under one year	12	8	20
Between 1-5 years	33	21	54
Between 6-10 years	24	15	39
Between 11-15 years	13	9	21
16 years and over	1	2	3
Total	83	54	137

Juvenile police records in most cases do not include the occupation or income of these families. However, the officers interviewed were of the opinion that all of the 70 families could be grouped in the lower income bracket. Three of the 70 families were known to be receiving aid from the Bureau of Public Assistance at the time of police investigation, and in another five, adults were unemployed and without any source of income.

Source and Method of Complaint

Complaints regarding neglect of children in the community come to the attention of police both by direct observation and through referral by other individuals. In the group under analysis, the largest number of cases of neglect was detected by the police themselves. The table on the following page gives the distribution of the 70 cases of neglect by source of complaint and method of complaint.

Source of Complaint

Neglect complaints detected by police. --Police officers of the Juvenile Division and the other divisions encounter numerous types of situations all the twenty-four hours

TABLE 5

DISTRIBUTION OF NEGLECT CASES ACCORDING TO
SOURCE AND METHOD OF COMPLAINT

Source	By Telephone	Detected by police	In person	Total
Police		20		20
Neighbors	17			17
Landlady	9			9
Hospital	5			5
Parents	3			3
Child			3	3
Relative			1	1
Citizen	2		2	4
Attorney	1		1	2
Bus depot	2			2
Baby sitter	1			1
Anonymous	3			3
Total	43	20	7	70

of the day, every day of the week. They are the first to be contacted for accidents, thefts, burglary, murders, fights in the families or neighborhood, as they are the primary constitutional force for the protection of life and property and maintenance of law and order. Dependent, neglected, and abused children come to their attention directly in several ways. In this study, police detected twenty of the neglect cases. The following illustrations are some examples:

Illustration VIII (Neglect case detected by traffice police)

Traffic police observed that a car was parked for three hours with

four children, two boys and two girls, between the ages of 4-8 years,
There was no adult in the car. Upon questioning, they told the police
that they did not know whether their father was. The traffic police informed the juvenile police who immediately came over. After an un-
successful attempt to locate the father, the juvenile police left a note for
the father in the car and brought the children to the juvenile police headquarters. Further talks with the children revealed that the parents were
separated and the mother's whereabouts were not known. Soon the father
came over to the police station. He told police officers that he was out
of work and had gone to the employment agency and later to a bar to have
a few drinks.

Illustration IX (Neglect and unfit home condition detected by police)

Mrs. H. was suspected of "offering" (prostitution) and was arrested.
Arresting officers found two children, a boy, age four, and a girl, age three,
in the house, which was in a filthy condition. They contacted the juvenile
police, who came and took charge of the children. Neighbors were questioned and it was found out that the mother left the children alone for several
hours at a time. Often, she did not give them enough food and the children
were found looking for food in garbage cans. Neighbors also told the police
that she entertained men in the presence of the children, since she lived in
a one-room apartment. Police removed the children to the Juvenile Hall
and filed a petition on their behalf.

The following illustration is an example of the protective function of the juvenile
police.

Illustration X (Juvenile police observe children loitering in undesirable area at night)

Juvenile police, during their night patrol, observed three boys, between the ages of 10 and 12 years, walking around in Chinatown with shoe-
shine kits in their hands. They were trying to make a little extra money by
shoe-shining. Police talked to them and found that they were out with the
knowledge and permission of their parents. They were taken home to their
respective parents by the police officers, who counseled the parents regarding child molesters and undesirable characters in and around Chinatown,
particularly at night.

In these as well as other similar cases in the study, police were able to observe
the neglect conditions of children because of the nature and method of their operation.
In Illustration VIII, for example, the children in the parked car were detected because of
the round-the-clock patrolling duties. In another similar situation police found two children in a parked car on a hot afternoon who had become very sick because of the heat.

Their mother was located by the police in a nearby bar.

Illustration IX is a situation where police were able to detect neglect because of the authority they have to enter homes where crime is suspected. (One fourth of the twenty neglect cases detected by police were discovered when police were investigating or making an arrest of an adult for crime other than child neglect.) In Illustration IX and other similar cases, the neighbors were aware of the mother's activities and the fact that she was neglecting her children but they did not report this to the police until the police came to investigate and arrest her for prostitution.

Neighbors, however, are not indifferent to child neglect conditions, since the second largest number of complaints in the group under study were received from neighbors and landladies, who were also neighbors in most cases.

In summary, out of the 20 cases of neglect detected by the police, 17 were booked under Section 700b of the Welfare and Institutions Code and 3 were booked under Section 273a of the Penal Code of California. While both these charges, in the framework of law, are considered as misdemeanors, cases booked under Section 273a of the Penal Code are of a more serious nature because the parent's neglect has endangered the life or health of the child.

Neglect complaints made by neighbors. --Usually the largest numbers of complaints from any source regarding neglected children in the community come from neighbors and landladies. This was true of the group of cases under study. Twenty-six of the 70 neglect cases in this study were brought to the notice of the police by neighbors and landladies. Neighbors living in the same apartment house, rooming house, or adjoining homes are in a position to observe from day to day if children in a certain family are being left alone or are uncared for and neglected. When they observe such a situation existing over a period of time, they may report it to the police. There are some instances when neighbors who are not on very friendly terms with each other report exaggerated conditions of neglect or abuse of children to the police which really do not call for police interference or action. They may do this for various personal reasons. However, according to the police, such complaints are rare.

Sometimes, when making a complaint of neglect, neighbors either do not identify themselves, identify but let the police know that they do not wish to be involved with police investigation, or do not wish to be disclosed as a source of complaint. Police are careful in such instances to respect the neighbors' wishes. Similarly, relatives may not identify themselves where they report neglect situations to the police.

Other sources of complaint. --Hospitals and doctors are important sources of complaint in cases where neglect has caused physical injury to the child or where parents have neglected or delayed in giving medical care which has resulted in the child's condition becoming worse or dangerous and causing him unnecessary suffering. Another type of complaint received from the hospitals arises when the mother needs to be admitted for a physical or mental ailment and there is no one to take care of the children.

Five of the 70 neglect cases under study were reported by the hospitals.

In the neglect cases in which one parent complained about the other the parents were separated or divorced.

In three cases, adolescent children complained to the police about parent neglect. In one case, there was excessive drinking on the part of the mother and setpfather; in another the mother was a dope addict and led an immoral life and there was no father living in the house. In the third the mother was physically ill and not able to take care of her child.

In two additional cases, citizens (who were not neighbors of the child) complained to the police. In one case a fourteen year old girl was seen with a man who was an undesirable character, and in the other case a citizen had notices some children frequently looking for food in garbage cans.

The bus depots report cases to the juvenile police when minor children arrive in a bus without any adults and do not know where to go. They may loiter around or look lost and sooner or later come to the attention of the depot authorities. In two cases in the study, the fathers came late, to receive their children. In one instance the child's father misunderstood the arrival time of the bus, and in the other case the children had the name and address of their father who could not be located. Both situations, however, involved children under twelve years of age who needed to be taken care of even though for short periods of time.

A baby sitter reported in one case, when the parents of a three months old baby did not return for the baby for twenty-four hours; this baby sitter was hired for two hours only. In another case an attorney reported a case to the juvenile police of two girls, both under twelve years of age, who refused to live with their mother. She was separated from their father and had their custody. The mother became drunk frequently and did not cook food or look after them.

Method of Complaint

The majority of the complaints on child neglect are made to the police by telephone. A few complaints are made in person and fewer still by letter. Table 5 shows the method of complaint in the group of cases under study.

Complaints are made and received by the Juvenile Police Division during all hours of the day and night. When a complaint is received, it is important from the point of view of the juvenile police to find out the nature and seriousness of the neglect condition. This information helps the police to decide whether immediate action is required or if investigation can be made some time later during the day. If a complaint indicates that the parents or parent concerned often leave their children alone and are not giving them the care they need, police try to find out if the children are alone at the time when the complaint is being made. If they are not, the complaint is noted and the family is contacted some time during that day for an investigation. If the complaint indicates that the children are by themselves or are in physical danger or are witnessing the fight of drunken parents or immoral living conditions, the police investigate the situation immediately.

Investigation Procedure

Any complaint of neglect received between 8:00 A.M. and 4:00 P.M. is assigned to the investigation officers on duty. Complaints which come in after 4:00 P.M. and need immediate attention are received at the office and then broadcast on the two-way radio system which is attached to all police cars. The juvenile police cars cruising in the area are given the address and the nature of the complaint briefly and are asked to go there immediately, if the facts of the situation so require. Any complaint of neglect received after 4:00 P.M. which does not require immediate action is investigated the following morning. This plan is followed because there are fewer juvenile police officers on duty between 4:00 P.M. and 8:00 A.M. than between 8:00 A.M. and 4:00 P.M. The officers on duty after 4:00 P.M. are generally on cruising duty.

As mentioned earlier, all juvenile police officers work in plain clothes and travel in unmarked cars. Whatever the source of complaint might be, investigation begins by going to the address where the neglect condition is reported to be. If the parents or the guardians are in the house, the juvenile police identify themselves and ask to be admitted. The same method is followed if parents are absent but older children or other adults are in the house.

The focus of investigation of the juvenile police, as indicated by them and substantiated by the analysis, in any situation of neglect is to determine the nature and intensity of the neglect situation; whether or not it is a chronic condition of neglect, and the positive elements, if any, in the less serious situation. These are determined in the following manner.

Physical Condition of the Children

Juvenile police observe the physical condition of the children with reference to physical cleanliness, clothes, signs of skin or other ailments. Their experience is that in most chronic neglect situations which are of a serious nature, the child's physical condition is poor. If the children are scantily clothed and the clothes they have are dirty, if they show signs of not having been washed or cleaned for several days or have a rash on their bodies due to lack of cleanliness, the police consider this as indicative of neglect.

Physical Condition of the House

In homes where the children are in filthy condition, the house usually is littered with dirty clothes, dirty dishes, and empty cans and bottles. In some extreme cases, police find rotting food in the kitchen and urine and feces on the floor of the bathroom with the toilet clogged. In 24 cases in the study there were indications that both the children and the houses were in "very poor physical condition." The following case illustration is representative of such conditions.

Illustration XI (Poor Physical Condition of House Associated with Neglect)

A telephone call from a neighbor one afternoon informed the juvenile police of five children between the ages of eight years and five months being left alone in the apartment for several hours at a time and frequently overnight. Upon reaching the house, juvenile police found the house in a filthy condition. The kitchen was full of dirty dishes and there was no food of any kind in the house. There was a bottle of sour milk for the baby. The mother, Mrs. I., had been out since the previous day and the younger children were crying because they were hungry. All the children had scanty clothing, which was filthy. None of them was wearing shoes or socks. The baby was in a dripping wet diaper which was also soiled. The juvenile police, upon questioning the neighbors, found that a condition of neglect had existed for several months. Mrs. I. had a previous record of neglect and was under probation.

The following case illustrates extremely poor physical conditions.

Illustration XII (Physical Condition of the House Unfit for Human Habitation)

A landlady complained one afternoon about a mother neglecting and leaving her two children, aged one year and three years, alone for several hours and sometimes overnight. The juvenile police, upon reaching the house, found these two children running around in the house completely nude. They were in a filthy condition and it was obvious that they had not been washed for several days. There was about two inches of water all over the floor from a tap which had been left running. There was stale food in the kitchen and the house was littered with dirty clothes, empty cans and bottles, and garbage. The whole place had a very unpleasant odor. The mother, Mrs. J., who was away for a whole day, told the officers upon her return that she had not cleaned the house since she moved in two and a half years back. She had not washed her dishes for the past several weeks. Investigating officers reported that the place was unfit for human habitation.

When the physical condition of the house is extremely bad and the place is unfit for human habitation, police often take pictures of the house and use these when requesting legal action by the juvenile court. Their opinion is that in these cases the condition of the house is so unfit that it "has to be seen to be believed." Written descriptions of the house cannot adequately portray the condition.

Questioning the Parents or Guardians

If parents or guardians are present when juvenile police reach the scene of neglect, it is the practice to question them about the neglect condition. Police method of questioning is expected to be direct and to the point. As law enforcement agents covering large geographic areas, their time in each case is limited. As stated earlier, their main objective in questioning the parents, children, and neighbors is to find out how serious is the neglect condition and how long it has existed, and whether the parents are able and willing to do something about it.

Parents are questioned in the presence of their children. Juvenile police believe that children, especially the older ones who are neglected by parents who drink, lead immoral lives and indulge in other anti-social activities, are often aware of their parents' activities. The officers interviewed for this study also stated that many neglectful parents do not try to hide their activities from their children, and that under such circumstances police questioning of parents in the presence of the children can have no worse effect on the children than the neglect condition already has had. Questions relate to the existing neglect condition.

The parents are asked for their reasons for such a condition. This leads to such information as whether there are both parents in the family or only one parent, their source of income, any physical or mental disability on the part of either parent, and the like. In the group under study, the police were not able to question parents in 32 of the 70 cases for the following reasons.

TABLE 6

DISTRIBUTION OF NEGLECT CASES ACCORDING TO REASONS PARENTS WERE NOT AVAILABLE FOR QUESTIONING

Reason	Number of Families
Parents had been arrested for prostitution, murder, theft, and the like	10
Parents found too drunk at time of investigation to answer questions	12
Parents in hospital for physical or mental ill-health	10
Total	32

If parents are not available at the time of police contact, police try to obtain the information from children (if they are old enough to give the necessary information), neighbors, and relatives.

In 38 of the 70 cases, juvenile police were able to talk to the parents, either at the time of their first investigation of the complaint or on the following day. In 30 of these 38 cases, parents were present in the house when police made their first contact. In 8 cases, police left written messages asking the parents to contact them at the police station. In 6 out of these 8 cases, the police were obliged to remove the children to the Juvenile Hall temporarily, because the children were either too young to be left alone in the house or they had no other place to go until their parents could be found. In the other two cases, while the children were found alone, they seemed capable of taking care of themselves and were not in any physical danger.

Questioning the Children

Children who are thought to be old enough to answer questions are questioned about their parents' whereabouts, drinking habits, and activities. Children are questioned both in the absence as well as in the presence of their parents. Juvenile police officers interviewed stated that chronically neglected children are seldom shy or hesitant. They say quite frankly if they have enough food to eat, how often they are left alone, and whether the parents drink. The interviewees, however, observed that in cases in which the neglect is not severe and has not gone beyond the physical level and parent-child relationship has not been thwarted to any damaging degree, children defend their parents in whatever way they can. For example, in Illustration I the two boys, when questioned about their mother's activities, told the police that while their mother did go out frequently in the evenings with her boy friend, she always fixed their dinner for them before leaving. They were emphatic about the fact that she was a good mother and looked after them well.

While it is not possible to say how many children out of the group of 137 were questioned (this information was not available from the records), it is thought that the usual practice is for most of the children over the age of five years to be questioned by juvenile police officers in cases of neglect.

Questioning the Neighbors

As stated earlier, neighbors and landladies are frequently the source of complaint in neglect cases. If they identify themselves at the time of making the complaint, then they are questioned during the investigation about the parents' activities including the frequency of leaving their children alone and any other pertinent information they might give about the neglect condition. Some neighbors and landladies give this information voluntarily; others, for personal reasons, do not want to be associated with police questioning or testifying. It is police policy to respect the wishes of neighbors.

Decision Making

After the investigation is complete, juvenile police must decide what action they are going to take, an action which depends on the facts disclosed in a particular case. While it is not always possible for the police to get all the facts in their first investigation, they do try to establish the seriousness of the neglect condition and determine whether it is a chronic condition of neglect or only an isolated incident. Within the legal frame of reference, theoretically, there are two clear-cut classifications in which any complaint of neglect can be viewed. These are violation or nonviolation of the law. When violation is readily observable or obviously not occurring, the line of action for the police is simple. In practice, however, police frequently encounter what they call the "grey" situations in neglect cases. These are situations in which the law has been violated, often for the first time, but the children appear to be unharmed at least physically by the neglect condition. In such cases, the police use their discretion and decide what line of action would best serve the interest of the child. According to police, if there are some positive elements in the house and one or both parents show a desire and willingness to do something to ameliorate the neglect condition, the parent or parents may be counseled but not arrested.

An example of such a situation is Illustration I. In this case, there was violation of law on the part of the mother because she left her two boys under ten years of age without adult supervision, frequently in the evenings and occasionally overnight. The boys looked well taken care of in every other respect, so police decided to talk to the mother the next morning and see if she was willing to change the situation in any way. The mother was cooperative and willing to make arrangements for an adult to be with her boys when she left them alone. She also showed good understanding of the possible consequences of leaving the children alone. The police, therefore, "counseled and warned" the mother and terminated the case at that point.

The term "counseling" when used by juvenile police indicates advising the parents how their actions are causing neglect of their children and warning them that legal action will be taken against them if they do not improve the existing conditions. These parents are also warned that police will pay a surprise visit to check if they have improved their condition. Interviewees stated that in some instances juvenile police may pay a surprise visit to a particular family after a few weeks or so, but as a rule they do not have time to do so.

Decisions Regarding Parents

The following table shows the types of decisions taken by the police regarding parents with reference to the group of neglect cases under study.

Of the 50 neglect cases in which a decision was necessary, juvenile police in two out of five cases arrested the parents for neglect and removed the children to juvenile hall. In approximately three out of each five cases parents were counseled and warned; very seldom were parents referred to welfare agencies.

Factors in neglect cases causing arrest of parents. --When juvenile police come across certain kinds of neglect situations in which parental neglect has endangered life or health of the children concerned, they consider these as serious neglect situations. As stated earlier, such cases are booked under Section 273a of the Penal Code of California. Being law enforcement agents, police are obligated in these situations to take legal action against the parents, to remove the children to Juvenile Hall if necessary, and to

TABLE 7

DISTRIBUTION OF NEGLECT CASES ACCORDING TO DECISIONS
TAKEN BY POLICE REGARDING PARENTS

Type of Decision	Number of Families
Parents arested for neglect	20
Parents counseled and warned for neglect	28
Parents referred to welfare agencies	2
No decision necessary (parents in hospital for physical or mental illness)	10
No decision necessary (parents already arrested for charges other than neglect)	10
Total	70

file a petition on their behalf in the juvenile court. This was true in 15 out of the 20 cases where juvenile police arrested parents for neglect. Some of these cases were chronic neglect situations; others were not chronic but serious enough to call for police law enforcement action.

The following illustrations highlight the factors in neglect conditions which police consider when deciding that legal action against the parent is necessary.

Illustration XIII (Factors in neglect cases which lead to legal action)

In answer to a complaint of neglect made by a neighbor, juvenile police found five children, all under seven years of age, in an extremely filthy apartment. Dirty clothes and dishes were scattered all over the house, which was permeated by an intolerable odor. There was no food in the house. The children were all very scantily clothed and looked as though they had not been washed or cleaned for weeks. The neighbors who had complained, and others in the apartment building, informed the police that the father's whereabouts were not known and the mother, Mrs. K (who was not present when police officers went for investigation) was a very irresponsible person. She left the children, including a three month old baby, alone during the day as well as night. She was known to visit bars at night and became drunk every day. The oldest boy, when questioned, told the police that his mother never looked after the children and was out most nights.

Before making out a written charge juvenile police, as a routine, check with their central records office located on Georgia Street to discover if the family has a prior police record, and its nature. In this case they found that the mother had a prior neglect record and she was under probation for six months.

The juvenile police decided to book the case under Section 273a of the Penal Code. The filthy physical condition of the house and extreme negligence on the part of the mother appeared to be definitely harmful for the children, who were all under seven years of age. These children had not had enough food to eat or proper clothing to wear over a considerable length of time. The three month old infant was heard crying by the neighbors for long periods at a time. The neighbors believed that the child was not given enough milk. The police learned that the mother had already been given one chance to improve the conditions for her children.

The mother was arrested in this case and the children were removed to Juvenile Hall.[12] The mother was given 45 days jail sentence. After her release her children, who had been made wards of the court, were returned to her under probation for a period of six months.

Some neglect complaints may not be about chronic conditions, but of a single act of neglect of a serious nature that endangers the life and health of the children concerned. In such situations juvenile police also are obliged to take legal action, under Section 273a of the Penal Code. The following case illustrates such a situation.

Illustration XIV (Single act of neglect resulting in legal action)

A citizen telephoned the juvenile police one afternoon and reported that a three month old baby was in a locked car for over two hours and was crying hysterically. The car was very warm. Police arrived on the scene and, after a quick search, found the mother, Mrs. L., in a nearby bar in an intoxicated condition. She had a four year old daughter with her.

The police booked this case under Section 273a of the Penal Code. They did not know how often the mother did this and they did not investigate the case any further. However, just the facts of the incident as they saw it indicated that the mother had endangered the life of the baby. He could have died of heat exhaustion. She had also taken her four year old daughter to a bar and had become drunk in her presence.

The mother was arrested[13] in this case but was bailed out by her husband immediately after her case was processed. The two children, who were temporarily under police custody, were released to the joint custody of the mother and father.

Police practice is that if parents are intoxicated in the presence of their children, either in their homes or outside, with children accompanying them at the time of police contact or investigation, and the children's condition further indicates neglect, police arrest the parents. In three out of each five of the 70 cases in which parents were arrested for neglect, intoxication at the time of police contact and investigation was one of the charges. In these cases "counseling" or "warning" by police was out of the question because, under the law, police officers cannot leave juveniles with adults who are intoxicated. In such cases the children are removed to Juvenile Hall and their parents are arrested, either for violating Section 273a of the Penal Code or Section 700d of the Welfare and Institutions Code, depending on the other factors of neglect present in the case. Unless the neglect condition associated with drunkenness is thought to endanger the life or health of children, parents generally come out of jail in one or two days and the children are released to them from Juvenile Hall until the hearing of their case. This was true in 60 percent of the cases where parents were arrested for neglect and drunkeness in the presence of their children.

Drunkenness associated with neglect.--In the group of 70 cases of neglect under study, drunkenness was a problem in 38 families, or slightly more than half of the sample. The following table indicates this problem:

TABLE 8

DISTRIBUTION OF NEGLECT CASES ACCORDING TO
DRUNKENNESS IN FAMILIES

	Families	Drunkenness
Both parents	28	11
Mother only	39	25
Father only	3	2
Total	70	38

If the two groups of single-parent families are combined (mother only and father only), drunkenness as well as neglect was encountered in 27 of the 42 families, a higher incidence than for the total.

In the 30 cases in which parents were not arrested and juvenile police decision was necessary, 28 parents were counseled and warned. In the remaining two cases parents were referred to welfare agencies.

As stated earlier, a charge of neglect in accordance with the various sections of Welfare and Institutions Code and the Penal Code is based primarily on the type of neglect condition which exists in a particular case. Section 700b of the Welfare and Institutions Code is generally applied in cases where children are neglected or are without any adult care because of their parents' physical or mental illness. It is also applied in cases where the parents or parent leave the children alone for long periods of time but provide enough food and proper clothing. In some of these cases parents are found to visit bars and drink frequently but not in the presence of children. According to juvenile police, it is in cases like these that they try to avoid, as far as possible, taking any legal action. Through counseling and warning they try to make the parents aware of the fact that the act of neglecting their children is punishable by law and it is in their own and their children's welfare and interest that they give proper care to their children. Parents are also warned, if necessary, that if they continue to neglect their children and a complaint is received by the police for a second time, legal action would be taken against them.

Cases which terminate in counseling and warning. --The following are illustrations of the kind of neglect cases where police try to avoid taking legal action and terminate the case with "counseling and warning."

Illustration XV (Neglect condition not leading to legal action)

A baby sitter telephoned the juvenile police one afternoon and informed them that she was baby sitting for a three month old baby girl. The parents, Mr. and Mrs. M., had asked her the previous evening to look after the baby for a couple of hours at her house but they had not come to take the baby that night or the following morning. She had no address where she could contact the parents or any of their relatives. She thought the baby had been abandoned.

The juvenile police asked her to bring the baby over to the Juvenile Division, which she did. The police kept the baby in their office for a few hours but later took her to Juvenile Hall. In the evening the parents came over to the Juvenile Division to take the child. When police questioned the parents they admitted being intoxicated and unable to return to the baby sitter's house for their baby.

These parents were counseled and warned by the juvenile police, and the baby was released from Juvenile Hall to them. Juvenile police observed that the parents were repentent. They both seemed to be otherwise reasonably responsible persons and promised not to repeat their actions in the future. The police felt that they should be given another chance. The fact that the baby was left in the care of an adult and not by herself showed that her parents were not completely irresponsible.

Illustration XVI (Neglect condition not leading to legal action)

Juvenile police noticed four children between three and seven years in a parked car for three hours. Their efforts to locate the father having failed, the children were brought over to the Juvenile Division. On questioning them the older boy said that the father often goes out in the evenings to drink and leaves them at home. The father came to the police station within a couple of hours. He said he had gone to the employment agency as he was out of a job and later on had gone to a bar to have a couple of drinks. He was divorced from his wife.

Juvenile police released the children to the father after counseling and warning. They observed that he seemed a reasonably responsible person and was willing to take care of the children. He promised not to leave them alone for long hours and would arrange to leave them with a babysitter as soon as he started working.

Isolated and unintentional cases of neglect. -- Children in isolated and unintentional cases of neglect are given the necessary protection and their parents are counseled; warning is not necessary in these cases. The following cases illustrate such situations.

Illustration XVII (Unintentional neglect)

The Greyhound Bus Depot informed the juvenile police one afternoon that two children, aged 8 years and 6 years, had arrived on the Greyhound bus from Yuma, Arizona. They were to be met by their father in Los Angeles but no one had come to meet them. The children were tired and hungry and also scared. They had only a vague idea where their father lived. Police tried to locate the father but had no success.

They brought the children over to the station, fed them, and looked after them for a while and then took them to Juvenile Hall. They continued their efforts in the meantime to locate the father. At about 10:00 P.M. the father came to the police station to claim his children. On talking to him, they found that he had misunderstood his wife over the telephone and thought the children were arriving on a later bus reaching Los Angeles at 9:00 P.M. and so had gone to meet a later bus. He seemed a responsible person, was holding a steady job, and had made satisfactory arrangements for the children's stay in Los Angeles until his wife could come and join them. The children were released to the father.

The following is a case of an isolated incident of neglect.

Illustration XVIII (Isolated incident of neglect)

Traffic police spotted two children in a semi-residential area, a boy three years old and a two year old girl, walking by themselves with a dog. They picked them up and informed the Juvenile Police, who came and took charge of them. The children were too young to give any information about their address or parents.

Juvenile police kept them at their station for some time and took care of them. After a couple of hours the mother, Mrs. N., contacted the police over the telephone.

She was asked to come down to the police station to claim the children, which she did. She explained that the children were playing in the neighbor's yard and had wandered off on their own. The children were released to her and no further action was taken.

In both these instances, neglect was an isolated incident and obviously unintentional. No investigation was made by the juvenile police, though the necessary protection was offered to the children. These cases were recorded under Section 700b, Welfare and Institutions Code.

Some neglect cases initially booked under 700b of the Welfare and Institutions Code can be changed to Section 700d of the code if investigation reveals that the neglect condition is chronic or more severe than it had appeared and for these reasons the home is unfit for the children. Similarly, cases booked under 700d may be changed to Section 273a of the Penal Code if investigation shows that parents have endangered the life or health of children.

Only two cases in the group were referred to welfare agencies. In one case the parents were having some marital problems and as a result were leaving their children alone for long periods during the day. In the other case there was financial problem in the family. Due to various reasons which are discussed in the final chapter, the juvenile officers interviewed stated that they are hesitant to refer cases to welfare agencies.

Neglect cases not requiring juvenile police decision. --No decision was necessary on the part of the juvenile police regarding the parents in the 10 cases where they were in hospital for physical or mental illness. Children in these cases were dependents (as well as neglected) and booked under Section 700b of the Welfare and Institutions Code. They were admitted temporarily to Juvenile Hall. If necessary, arrangements are made for their foster home placement by the juvenile police in consultation with Juvenile Hall, until such time as the parent is recovered and is able to take care of them.

In the last group of 10 cases, while the children were brought to the attention of juvenile police after their parent or parents had already been arrested for reasons other than neglect, investigation was made by the juvenile police in each case to find out if the children were exposed to immoral or other unfit home conditions. Investigation revealed that in 7 cases parents had exposed their children to immoral living conditions such as drinking, gambling, or prostitution. In one of these cases children had witnessed their parents becoming drunk and the subsequent murder of the father by the mother with a knife. These cases were booked under Section 700d of the Welfare and Institutions Code. The other three were booked under Section 700b of the code; parents in these cases were arrested for drunk driving or for being found drunk on the road, and police investigation did not reveal any physical neglect of children.

Decisions Regarding Children

The juvenile police have a limited choice in making decisions regarding the temporary care of the neglected children until the juvenile court can come to a decision about their guardianship and placement. Neglected and dependent children in the group of families under study were placed in temporary care by the police in the following ways.

TABLE 9

DISTRIBUTION OF NEGLECT CASES ACCORDING TO
TEMPORARY PLACEMENT OF CHILDREN

Placement	Number of Families
Juvenile Hall (Lathrop)	48
Placed in foster homes	2
Left with or returned to parents	15
Left with relatives	4
Left with neighbors	1
Total	70

Admitting children to Juvenile Hall. --Children are temporarily admitted to Juvenile Hall if the parents are physically or mentally ill or arrested for any crime and there is no relative available and willing to take care of them. Children who are in a serious physical neglect condition or are living in an unfit home are also admitted to Juvenile Hall, whether the parents are arrested on the spot or not. Generally, where serious neglect conditions are endangering life and health of children, parents are arrested, but they may not always be available on the spot. In minor neglect situations where the police decide that counseling and warning the parents might help, but the children are alone and the parents are out, juvenile police take the children to Juvenile Hall if the parents do not return within a reasonable period of time. In such cases, police leave a note at the home address for the parents and first take the children to their Juvenile Division headquarters. If parents do not come or contact the police within a reasonable period of time, then the children are taken to Juvenile Hall for a temporary period or until such time as the parents are contacted.

Under any of the circumstances outlined above, when children are taken to Juvenile Hall for detention, police officers interviewed state that they explain to the children, if they are old enough to understand, where they are being taken and for what reason. They explain to them that in Juvenile Hall there are other children of their age for them to play with. They have school and many recreational facilities and they will be happy there. They also explain to them that they will stay there until their parents can be located or helped or come out of jail, depending on what the circumstances of the parents are.

Interviews with juvenile police officers indicated that, in their experience, children who are often left to themselves by their parents or are neglected in other ways seldom show signs of being upset or scared when told about going to the Juvenile Hall. They seem to accept it in a matter-of-fact manner and, while some children may ask a few questions about their parents or the length of time they will stay at the Juvenile Hall and the like, most of them do not.

Before the children are taken to Juvenile Hall the juvenile police telephone the Juvenile Hall authorities to find out if they have a vacancy to admit the child concerned. If they have, the officers prepare the children. If they are in bed or ready for bed they are changed into other available clothing; if they are taken first to the juvenile police station, officers provide them with food or drink if necessary. If some children are upset and cry or are scared in any way they are comforted. Whatever the situation, juvenile police try to make the children comfortable and take care of their needs until they take them to Juvenile Hall. After they are admitted, the Juvenile Hall management is responsible for the child's care until he is released.

In cases where the neglect is not of a serious nature and the police think that counseling and warning or referral to a welfare agency might help, children are generally left with their parents. However, in these instances, the parents are either present when the police go to investigate or return while they are there. Because detention of children is for protective and not for punitive reasons, juvenile police explore the possibilities of leaving children in the care of neighbors or relatives, if they volunteer to do so, until the parents arrive. This arrangement is considered suitable only in cases of mild neglect or dependency where the child is not in physical danger of any kind and the juvenile police are convinced that the neighbor or relative is willing and able to care for the child in the parents' absence. If they have any doubts they take the child to Juvenile Hall.

Temporary care in foster homes.--A very small number of foster homes licensed by the Bureau of Public Assistance are also available for temporary care and shelter of the dependent and neglected children, particularly children under the age of five years.[14] Police officers interviewed for this study stated that they hope further facilities in foster care will develop in the near future so that the younger children may receive better care.

Admitting children to the County General Hospital.--In some cases, children are admitted to the Los Angeles County General Hospital. These children are either in need of medical care or are young infants who are not admitted to the Juvenile Hall nursery because of lack of room. As mentioned earlier, this nursery is equipped to accommodate only twenty-three children and frequently has no vacancies.

Filing petitions on behalf of children.--Juvenile police make a request for a petition in the juvenile court on behalf of those children who are admitted to Juvenile Hall because of unfit home conditions or serious neglect by parents. In the group of 70 families under study, petition was requested by police in 33 cases. These petitions are based on the facts of neglect or unfit home conditions which the police find after investigation.

In cases where the physical condition of the home has deteriorated excessively, petitions are accompanied with photographs which the police take at the time of investigation to support the facts stated in the petition and to help the juvenile court to visualize the conditions existing in a particular home.

Petitions must be submitted to the juvenile court within forty-eight hours or two court days (excluding Saturdays, Sundays, or legal holidays) of the children's admission to Juvenile Hall. Detention of children is temporary; if it is not under court order or a petition is not submitted within the limited time, children are released to their parents. After receiving a petition, the juvenile court arranges for a pre-detention hearing within the next twenty-four hours. On the basis of the facts stated in the investigation report, the juvenile court judge decides whether the children should be detained in Juvenile Hall until the date of hearing of their case or may stay with parents or relatives. While the judge's decision, one way or the other, in most cases depends on the condition of the home and parents as stated in the investigation report, in severe neglect and unfit home condition the children are seldom returned to live at home until after the hearing of the case. In most of these cases parents have been arrested. However, children may be released and allowed to stay at home with parents if the judge thinks that the existing neglect condition is not harmful for the children.

The time limit of forty-eight hours within which the juvenile police must submit their petition is in itself a limiting factor in the method of police operation in the neglect situations. It means that their investigation of a particular case must be complete within this period and the petition should give all the pertinent facts. Detailed investigation of most neglect cases is done during the day even though the complaint might have been made and attended to the previous evening or night. The reason for this is that while there are only two juvenile officers on patrol duty in this areas between 4:00 P.M. and 1:15 A.M., there are at least six investigation officers in a geographic area the size of the Central Division during the day. Besides, in the daytime it is usually easier to contact relatives, neighbors, and others who might verify that neglect conditions exist.

It is not always possible for the juvenile police to obtain all the facts about a case in one visit. In many situations they are unable to meet the neighbor or relative who lodged the complaint when they go to the address for the first time. Often, after a busy weekend, there are too many juvenile cases of neglect and delinquency to be investigated within the specified time. The forty-eight-hour limit is applicable to all juveniles under detention, including the delinquents. The result is that detailed investigation is not always possible. Police officers interviewed stated that if they had more time they could study some of the cases in more detail before filing the petition.

The Juvenile Records Office is open twenty-four hours a day, which makes it possible for a juvenile officer in any part of the city, at any time of the day or night, to find out within minutes if a particular case of juvenile neglect, dependency, or abuse has had a previous police contact and, if so, the date and nature of the offense. The officer requests and receives this information over the two-way radio system in his car. Information about previous contacts of a case is helpful to the juvenile officers in deciding their line of action.

Terminating Contact with Cases

The police work rapidly within the framework of law enforcement. Whatever the decision regarding any neglect situation, juvenile police contact with the family terminates within a few hours in most cases and within two days for all but a few exceptional cases. The initial decision as to whether or not the law has been broken is immediate in most situations of neglect.

In cases of mild neglect the parents are counseled and contact is terminated. In cases of extreme neglect where the parents are arrested and the children removed to Juvenile Hall, the juvenile police complete the investigation on the spot or within the following twenty-four hours and make their formal report. They then file a request for legal action with the juvenile court within forty-eight hours of placing the children in Juvenile Hall.

The police do not have to attend the juvenile court hearing unless the parents in a case do not accept the allegation of neglect and unfit home conditions made by the investingating officers.

The Juvenile Police Division receives a green slip from the juvenile court after the hearing is completed, indicating the disposition of the case.

Footnotes

[1] Webster's New International Dictionary, Second Edition, 1957.

[2] Henry Campbell Black, Black's Law Dictionary (Minnesota: West Publishing Co., 1951), p. 1,184.

[3] Ibid., p. 1184.

[4] Ibid.

[5] Ibid.

[6] Vincent DeFrancis, Child Protective Services in the United States, A Nationwide Survey (Denver: Children's Division, The American Humane Association, 1956), Ch. V.

[7] The term "booked" is used by the juvenile police to indicate that a charge was entered in their records for a case. The term is used in this study to indicate the same meaning.

[8] Misdemeanor is a legal offense of less gravity than a felony. Every offense declared to be a misdemeanor is punishable by imprisonment in the county jail, not exceeding $500.00, or six months, or both.

[9]A part of Juvenile Hall (Detention Home) of Los Angeles County where dependent or neglected children are housed separately from delinquent children. Lathrop Hall has a nursery section which accommodates children up to three years of age. Boys and girls between the age of 3 and 18 years have separate living arrangements. Facilities for schooling, recreation, and medical care are available for the children. While the nursery section was made to house 21 children and the older children's section 60 boys and girls, as many as 140-150 children have to be accommodated sometimes. In this study, the term Juvenile Hall is used wherever the Lathrop Section of Juvenile Hall is involved. Recently, McLaren Hall has been added as an additional facility for temporary care of neglected and abused children.

[10]The word "petition" is generally used in judicial proceedings to describe an application in writing in contradition to a motion which may be viva voce. In child neglect and abuse cases, petitions to the Juvenile Court are filed by the Probation Department. However, juvenile Police make an application for petition or legal action on the basis of facts of neglect and abuse obtained through observation and investigation. In this study, "filing a petition" is used to indicate a request made by juvenile police for legal action.

[11]The number of Oriental and American Indian families in the population of the district was very low, though the exact number was not available. This information was secured from the Central Division and is based on the latest figures available in 1959, from the Planning and Research Division of the Los Angeles Police Department.

[12]The procedure followed in removing the neglected children to Juvenile Hall is discussed later in this chapter.

[13]When the available facts in a neglect situation indicate that parents should be arrested and children removed to Juvenile Hall, the investigating officers contact the sergeant on duty in the Juvenile Division of the area concerned. If he is not available then the watch commander on duty is contacted.

[14]Eugene W. Barnett, "A Survey of Ten Families Whose Children Were Emergently Placed by the Police in Subsidized Foster Homes" (unpublished Master's thesis, University of Southern California, 1961).

CHAPTER V

ANALYSIS OF CASES OF ABUSE

Juvenile police investigated 72 cases of child abuse in the Central Division during 1958. The files on all these cases were studied but only 30 cases, or somewhat less than 50 percent, were selected for detailed study; the criterion for selection being the availability of the officer responsible for the case.

This chapter contains an analysis of these 30 cases and includes a brief discussion illustrating the possible forms which child abuse may take and the sections of the Penal Code under which the juvenile police may act. The analysis takes the form of classification of the cases within headings such as age, sex, and race of child, method and source of complaint, and an examination of the juvenile police investigation procedure and decision making.

Child Abuse

Legislation to protect children from adult abuse and cruelty is to be found in every state.[1] These laws differ in form from state to state. In the State of California, children under 18 years of age are protected from adult abuse by various sections of the Penal Code which fall under classifications such as child annoyance or molestation, indecent exposure, incest, rape, six crimes against children, child beating, wilful cruelty, and endangering life or health of children and immoral practices in the presence of children. Sections of the Penal Code relevant to this study are given in Appendix A.

The 30 cases selected for this study fall under the two broad categories of sex offense and child beating, in the ratio of 23 to 7, respectively. Most sex offenses against children, and all child-beating offenses, are felony[2] cases. It should be pointed out here that the total number of child beating cases for the year and area under study was seven and that, by chance, the investigating officers in all seven were available for interviews; hence all seven cases are included in the selected group of 30 cases. This results in a distortion of the sample but does not conceal the fact that sexual abuse is numerically the most common form of child abuse within the group. This fact was indicated by the officers interviewed and is substantiated by the sample.

In the following pages, 23 cases of sex abuse of children are considered first, followed by 7 cases of child beating.

Sexual Abuse of Children

Like any other form of crime, sex crimes against children vary in degree of severity and range anywhere from "mild annoyance" to "rape." The following table shows the distribution of 23 cases under study, as booked under various charges.

TABLE 10

DISTRIBUTION OF SEX ABUSE CASES ACCORDING TO TYPE OF CHARGE

Type of Charge	Number of Cases
Section 647a, Penal Code	5
Section 288, Penal Code	17
Section 261.1, Penal Code	1
Total	23

Cases Booked Under Section 647a of the Penal Code

The following illustrations are representative of sexual abuse cases which are booked under Section 647a(i) of the Penal Code. These are generally cases of "mild annoyance."

Illustration XIX (Mild Annoyance)

The manager of a movie house telephoned the juvenile police about an adult who was annoying an eleven year old girl. Police reached the movie house and found that this girl was watching the show by herself. A man about thirty-three years old, who was sitting next to her, annoyed her by first talking to her, then putting his hand on her lap and tickling her. She changed her seat a few times but he followed her around. Finally, she left the hall and reported the matter to the usher, who informed the manager.

When police questioned the man he admitted talking to her but said he did not intend to harm her. The man was first arrested under Section 647a(i) of the Penal Code but was released within a short time because the annoyance was of a minor nature and he did not have a prior police record.

The following case illustrates a similar case which resulted in the arrest of the offender.

Illustration XX (Annoyance Leading to Arrest)

Traffic police observed a 16 year old girl running in the MacArthur Park and a middle aged man following her at about 12:30 P.M. When the girl saw the police car, she shouted for help. The police reached her immediately. The girl told the police that while she was sitting on a bench, this man came and sat next to her and asked her if she would go swimming with him. When she refused him he moved closer to her and put his arms around her. She jumped from her seat and starting running. He followed her; when a man questioned him he told him that she was his wife. The girl saw the police car in time to call for help.

Police arrested this man, who tried to run in the opposite direction when he saw the police. He pleaded guilty and was booked under 647a of the Penal Code.

In both these cases, the offense was of a minor nature and no physical harm was done to the juveniles concerned. The following examples illustrate cases of a more serious nature.

Cases of Sexual Abuse of Boys Booked Under Section 288
of the Penal Code

Illustration XXI (Sexual Abuse of a Boy)

Police were called when a seven year old boy who went to the men's toilet in a park at about 2:00 P.M. was molested by a seventy-one year old man. Investigation revealed that another man, who came into the toilet, found that this little boy was crying; he was held down by force by the older man was was masturbating himself while playing with the boy's private parts. This man caught the older man and held him in custody with the help of one of the officers of the park until police came.

The suspect was arrested by the police and was booked under Section 288 of the Penal Code.

Illustration XXII (Sexual Abuse of Several Boys by One Adult)

A citizen informed the juvenile police that an adult in his middle thirties was taking several young boys, between the ages of 10-12 years, to his apartment for homosexual activities. Police went to the address given and found five youngsters, all under twelve years of age, sitting in a dark room along with suspect and watching television. Police questioned the suspect about the complaint but he denied any homosexual activity on his part. However, all the boys admitted being molested by suspect in return for having cokes and letting them watch television.

The suspect was arrested and booked under Section 288 of the Penal Code.

In the group of 23 cases, there were five cases of homosexuality where boys between the ages of 7 and 12 years were molested by adults between the ages of 60 and 70 years. All of the five adults were single males living alone.

Interviews and discussions with juvenile police officers indicated that homosexual activities of older men with boys under twelve years of age are a common form of sex abuse of children which the juvenile police encounter in this city. Most of these men are found to be single, living by themselves in apartments or rooming houses. They offer money, candies, or cokes as temptation to entice the children to their living quarters.

In the remaining 18 cases, girls were victims of sexual abuse of male adults. All these cases were booked under the various sections of the Penal Code, depending upon the nature of the offense.

Cases of Sexual Abuse of Girls Booked Under Section 288 of the Penal Code

Illustration XXIII (Sexual Molestation of a Four Year Old Girl)

The mother of a four year old girl telephoned the police and said that her daughter had been molested. Investigation revealed that the girl was asked by an elderly man about 68 years old to go to his apartment. He promised to give her candies. He was a neighbor and the girl was acquainted with him. When she went in he locked the door, pulled down her panties and fondled her private parts. Afterwards he kissed her, gave her candies, and asked her not to tell anyone what he had done.

The girl was frightened and told her mother, who informed the police. The suspect first denied the charges but pleaded guilty later. He was arrested and booked under Section 288 of the Penal Code.

The following illustrations are examples of molestation and abuse of older girls.

Illustration XXIV (Sexual Molestation of an Eleven Year Old Girl)

An eleven year old girl went to her mother crying and looking very scared and told her that a man in the neighborhood called her in his apartment as she was returning from school, saying he wanted to show her something interesting. When she went in, he threw her down on the couch and started fondling her private parts. The girl screamed and ran out. The girl's mother informed the police.

When the offender was questioned by the police he pleaded guilty and admitted that he wanted to molest the girl but she did not let him. He was arrested under Section 288 of the Penal Code.

Illustration XXV (Sexual Abuse of a Girl)

A ten year old girl went to baby-sit, with the permission of her parents, for a couple who were their ex-neighbors. Before leaving the house the man (ex-neighbor) found the girl alone in the living room and his wife busy in the garage; he kissed the girl and started fondling her private parts and attempted to insert his finger in her vagina. When the girl protested and cried, he threatened to beat her. Before leaving, he told her not to tell anyone about it, otherwise he would "beat the life" out of her. As soon as he left with his wife in the car, the girl ran out and went to a nearby gas station. She telephoned her mother and aunt from there. Her aunt, who lived close by, came over immediately. She called the police from the gas station and was able to give the description of the man and his car registration number.

Police placed an "all units"[3] call and thus alerted the patrolling cars in the city to be on the lookout for his car. He was located and arrested within an hour. The girl was taken to the hospital for a medical examination, which indicated "recent injuries to the external genitalia and deflorated hymen." There was no bleeding.

The suspect at first denied all charges. However, he pleaded guilty when the girl identified him at the police station as the person who had molested her. He was arrested and booked under Section 288 of the Penal Code.

These three cases are illustrative of adult sexual abuse against juvenile girls. Police observation is that there are very few instances of rape of girls below the age of fourteen. Girls between the ages of 14-18 years, who are classed as rape victims, often come under "statutory rape" covered under Section 261.1 of the Penal Code, the violation of which is a felony. The following case illustrates this type of abuse. This is the only case of statutory rape in the group under study.

Case of Sexual Abuse Booked Under Section 261.1
of the Penal Code

Illustration XXVI (Statutory Rape)

An anonymous caller one night informed the police that an adult male had checked in a downtown hotel with a girl who looked like a juvenile and perhaps was not his wife. Police reached the spot immediately and found a fifteen year old girl in bed with an adult who was in his middle thirties. Both admitted having had sexual intercourse. Suspect pleaded guilty and said he was aware of the girl's age and knew he might get caught. However, the act was committed with the consent of the girl.

Investigation revealed that he was the girl's brother-in-law (husband of step-sister). The girl had no permanent home. She had no father and her mother, who was her legal guardian, was out of town with the girl's stepfather. The girl had been living with her step-sister and her husband for the last year. Earlier, she had lived with some other relatives. Police arrested the suspect and booked him under Section 261.1 of the Penal Code.

Factual Information

Racial Origin

The racial origin of the 23 cases under study is as follows:

TABLE 11

DISTRIBUTION OF SEXUAL ABUSE CASES ACCORDING TO RACIAL ORIGIN

Racial Origin	Number of Cases
Caucasian	18
Negro	2
Mexican	3
Total	23

A total of 23 children were victims of sexual abuse in the 23 cases; they were 5 boys and 18 girls. Their distribution according to age group is shown in the following table.

TABLE 12

DISTRIBUTION OF SEXUAL ABUSE CASES ACCORDING TO AGE AND SEX OF CHILDREN

Age Group	Boys	Girls	Total
Under 1 year	-	-	-
Between 1-5 years	-	2	2
Between 6-10 years	3	9	12
Between 11-15 years	1	4	5
16 years and over	1	3	4
Total	5	18	23

Source and Method of Complaint

Source

Unlike cases of neglected children where complaint is made by persons other than parents, in cases of sexual abuse juvenile police report that the majority of the complaints are made by parents. In this study, approximately two thirds of the complaints of sexual abuse were made by parents.

The following table indicates the source of complaint in the 23 cases.

In three instances the police spotted the cases. One is described in Illustration XX. In the other two cases, juvenile police, while cruising in the evening, observed juvenile boys in a park in the company of adults who had prior records of violation of Section 288 of the Penal Code. In both cases suspects admitted homosexual activities with the juveniles and were arrested.

Citizens and neighbors made complaints to the police in two cases in which sexual abuse of children was suspected.

TABLE 13

DISTRIBUTION OF SEXUAL ABUSE CASES ACCORDING
TO SOURCE OF COMPLAINT

Source of Complaint	Number of Cases
Parents	16
Spotted by police	3
Citizen	2
Anonymous	2
Total	23

Method

All complaints in this group were made to the juvenile police by telephone except in three cases where the police spotted the cases.

Investigation Procedures

Immediate Attention

The juvenile police practice is to attend to the complaints of child abuse immediately because of the nature of the offense. Any sexual crime against a child, whether it is a felony or a misdemeanor, calls for police action against the offender. Immediate action is necessary in all cases of sex abuse even if the child is not physically hurt, in order to be able to locate the offender and gather all available evidence. The focus of investigation of the juvenile police in child abuse cases is to prosecute the offender; their activities with reference to the offender are with this objective.

Complex Nature of Investigation

The investigation of sexual abuse cases present a complex problem. In neglect and child beating cases, juvenile police have tangible evidence of the condition, even in the less serious cases. In sexual abuse cases, on the other hand, unless the abuse has caused physical injury, the only substantial evidence which the police have is the child's statement about how he or she was molested. If the child is upset or disturbed (as they are in many cases) it becomes even more difficult for the police to obtain an accurate account of the incident. Though sexual molestation of children is a felony, the police need an accurate account of the incident from the child in order to be able to make a case for a felony charge; in some cases it is necessary for the child to given an equally accurate account of the incident in the District/City Attorney's Office; otherwise, the criminal charge made by the police is not accepted by the District/City Attorney for lack of evidence.

Cases of sexual abuse in which pre-school age children are involved present a more difficult problem than others, from the juvenile police point of view. These children, being very young, often forget the details of the incident between the time of occurrence and the date of hearing. The following case is an illustration of such a situation.

Illustration XXVII (Sexual abuse case which could not be proved)

A woman in her early thirties complained to the juvenile police that her two daughters, aged four and seven, had been molested by her boy friend. The girls had complained to the mother that when she was away from the house for some work the suspect, a man of about 39 years, fondled the girls' private parts and asked them to fondle his.

At the time of police investigation the incident had just happened and both the girls were able to state clearly all the facts. However, at the district attorney's office the girls had to wait for a long period of time in the waiting room before their case came up. The older girl did not give a very accurate account of the incident. The younger sister became tired and sleepy. Medical examination had not given any indication of physical injury. Under these circumstances, the district attorney could not issue a criminal complaint, so the suspect was released, although the juvenile police and the mother believed the suspect to be guilty of molesting the girls.

Questioning the Child and His Parents

When a complaint of sexual abuse of a child is received, the juvenile police first contact the child and his parents or whoever has complained. They question the child and his parents as to the nature of the offense, time, place, and person associated with it. Juvenile officers interviewed indicated that they try to talk to the children patiently so as to be able to get an accurate account of the incident. This is not always possible, particularly when the parents are present and are upset about what has happened to their child. Often such parents also demand the something should be done immediately to punish the offender. Under such circumstances the children also get upset and the investigation slows down.

Medical Examination

If the facts in a case indicate that a medical examination or treatment is necessary, the child is taken to the hospital immediately. In some ca es, medical treatment may not be necessary and therefore not so important as the medic 1 examination in order to find out the nature and extent of the abuse. Juvenile police take the child to the hospital for the necessary medical examination, treatment, and report if the parents have not already done so. Parents can, if they wish, take the child to their own private doctor. However, the juvenile police in all abuse cases obtain a medical report on the abused condition. In the group of eighteen cases of sexual abuse of girls, medical treatment was necessary in two cases for minor injuries. In six others, a medical examination was given but no treatment was necessary.

Locating the Suspect

Attempts are made by the police to locate the suspect as soon as possible. If a suspect is a resident of the same neighborhood, it is easy to locate him. Because of the nature of the offense, the offenders seek privacy for molesting the children, either in their own apartment or in apartments where the children live, if parents are away. When the offense is committed in parks or places other than apartments, police try to locate the suspects with the help of the physical description which the child and others might give. However, there are instances where molestation or annoyance occurs on a lonely street and the suspect is able to get away from the neighborhood before the police can arrive. Such instances are said to be few and in the group of cases under study police were able to locate all the suspects.

Decision Making

Decisions Regarding Offenders

According to the nature and the seriousness of the abuse and the available facts, the suspect is arrested either on a misdemeanor charge or on a felony charge. [4] The victim (child) must be able to identify the suspect as the person who molested him or her before the police make an arrest. This is done frequently at the juvenile police station, where the child is taken either by the juvenile police or by his parents. If the suspect happens to be a neighbor or lives in the same apartment building as the child, police take the child to his apartment for identification just before arresting him.

In the group of 23 cases under study, all the suspects (offenders) were males between the ages of 21-70 years. The following table shows their distribution according to age.

If the offender's crime is charged as a misdemeanor, but he has had a prior record of sexual abuse of a child, major or minor, his offense is considered a felony. In the group under study, 8 offenders were booked under a felony charge because they had previous records of child molestation. As soon as a suspect is located, juvenile police check by radio with the Juvenile Record Division (where records of all arrests of adults booked for crimes committed against children are kept) to discover if the offender has a previous record.

TABLE 14

DISTRIBUTION OF SEXUAL ABUSE CASES ACCORDING TO AGE OF OFFENDERS

Age Group	Number of Adults
Between 20-30 years	5
Between 31-40 years	6
Between 41-50 years	5
Between 51-60 years	-
Between 61-70 years	7
Total	23

Type of Punishment.--In the group of 23 cases, 17 cases were classed as felony and 6 cases as misdemeanor. The following table shows the type of punishment given to the offenders under these two classifications.

TABLE 15

DISTRIBUTION OF SEXUAL ABUSE CASES ACCORDING TO TYPE OF PUNISHMENT GIVEN TO OFFENDERS

Type of Punishment	Felony	Misdemeanor	Total
90 days jail sentence	10	-	10
30 days jail sentence	7	-	7
15 days jail sentence	-	1	1
Fined	-	1	1
Warned by juvenile police	-	4	4
Total	17	6	23

Offenders frequently plead "not guilty" in sex abuse cases, especially where no physical injury has been caused to the child and the charges are filed only on the basis of the child's story. In such cases juvenile police are required to attend the hearing and given written and verbal testimony of the child's account of the incident, his reactions to the experience as they saw it, and his ability to describe and identify the suspect.

Decision Regarding Children

Children in these cases are often left with their parents or guardians after the juvenile police have helped them to get the necessary medical attention and obtained all the facts of the incident. However, if the crime is committed by a parent who is living in the same house as the child, police might decide to remove the child to the Juvenile Hall. In the group under study, children in all cases except one were left with their parents. In one case the girl was a victim of statutory rape by her brother-in-law. She was temporarily admitted to Juvenile Hall until her mother, who was out of town, came back.

Terminating Contact with Cases

Juvenile police terminate their contact with these cases after filing a complaint against the offender and, in some cases, after appearing at the court hearing to testify. If the offender pleads "not guilty" and further investigation is necessary, the police remain active with the case until the necessary facts are gathered and presented to the court. Their contact with the child terminates after they obtain details of the case from him and medical reports from the hospital where necessary.

Child Beating

The 7 child beating cases analyzed in this study were booked for violation of Section 27sd of the Penal Code. Two cases (Illustrations XXVIII and XXIX) were booked for violation of Section 273a of the Penal Code as well, because the beating and cruelty inflicted on the children were severe enough to endanger their life and limb.

The following cases illustrate severe child abuse and beating situations encountered by the juvenile police.

Cases Booked Under Sections 273a and 273d of the Penal Code

Illustration XXVIII (Severe physical abuse and cruelty)

A doctor from the Los Angeles County General Hospital telephoned the juvenile police about a five week old baby boy who had been severely abused physically by his parents. Investigation revealed that Mr. and Mrs. R., who were in their early thirties, lived in common law relationship. They both drank excessively and quarreled often. Neither of them was steadily employed. The crying of the infant irritated the father very much. His method of quieting the infant was to place a big pillow on his face. He had frequently threatened to kill the baby. While the mother was out one afternoon to a movie, having left the baby in the father's care, the father became drunk. When the baby woke up and started crying, the father lifted him up and dropped him on the floor a few times. The mother, on her return, found the child in a very bad condition but she did not do anything about it until the following morning, when she took him to the hospital. The doctor found that the infant had eight broken ribs, besides several cuts and bruises on his body. Parents stated that he was an "unwanted child."

Juvenile police investigation of neighbors showed that both parents had been maltreating the infant since his birth and he was heard crying constantly. Both parents were arrested for violation of Sections 273a and 273d of the Penal Code.

Illustration XXIX (Brutal beating)

The manager of the apartment where Mr. and Mrs. S. lived telephoned the juvenile police one night and reported that the couple were drunk and the father had brutally beaten his six year old son with his belt. Police reached the spot and found the child had several cuts and bruises on his body and was bleeding all over. The father admitted beating the boy because he was angry with him. Investigation from neighbors revealed that both parents were frequently drunk and had violent fights in the presence of their six children who were between the ages of one and nine years. The father often beat the children brutally. He also beat his wife when he was drunk. Children were left unsupervised by parents for several hours at a time. The father's sister, who lived close by and knew this family's condition, told the police that these parents neglected the children and were cruel to them. The father was known to have molested his nine year old daughter twice.

Police removed the six year old boy first to the Central Receiving Hospital and later to the Los Angeles General Hospital for observation. The other children were removed to Juvenile Hall. A petition was filed in the juvenile court on their behalf for their care. Both parents were arrested; the father for child beating under Section 273d of the Penal Code and the mother for endangering life and limb of children under Section 273a of the Welfare and Institutions Code.

These two cases represent the extreme type of cruelty and beating. The following illustrations of cruelty and child beating cases are less severe but, as indicated by the officers interviewed, they are encountered by the police more often than the severe ones.

Cases Booked Under Section 273d of the Penal Code

Illustration XXX (Severe beating)

Mr. T., the stepfather of an eleven year old girl, contacted the juvenile police and complained about his wife beating their daughter unmercifully that morning and on previous occasions. Police reached the address immediately and found physical signs of severe beating on the child's body. She was removed to Central Receiving Hospital immediately for medical care and later to Juvenile Hall. The father and daughter told the juvenile police of similar beating on previous occasions. The mother admitted to the juvenile police that she beat the girl cruelly when she was upset with the father. She was arrested under Section 273d of the Penal Code.

Illustration XXXI (Uncertain case of child beating)

Neighbors of Mr. and Mrs. V. complained one night to the juvenile police that Mr. and Mrs. V. often beat their two year old cruelly. Police, upon investigation, found the child with old discolored bruises on her face, arms, and body. Parents denied beating her and said that bruises were caused by her falling down several times while playing or running. However, police took the child to the Central Receiving Hospital to be examined because the neighbors had said that they had heard the child being beaten and crying. The doctor who examined the child at the hospital diagnosed the injuries to be old and was unable to say whether they were due to beating or falling accidentally. As the injuries were old and not serious, the child was returned to parents and they were warned about the consequences of child beating.

Juvenile police officers stated that they are more inclined to prosecute the parents or offenders in child beating cases, even when it is an isolated incident of beating, because it is an act of "commission" and punishable as a felony. However, for prosecution purposes, the injury resulting from a beating of the child must consist of severe bruises or lacerations. The spanking of a child by a father or mother which might produce discolorations of the skin is not considered to be a violation of the law. The injuries inflicted and the cause therefor must be unreasonable.

Factual Information About Child Beating Cases

Racial Origin

Six of the 7 families were Caucasian and one was Negro. A total of 12 children were the victims of beating and physical cruelty in these cases.

Age and Sex

The following table shows the age and sex of the 12 children.

TABLE 16

DISTRIBUTION OF CHILD BEATING CASES ACCORDING
TO AGE OF CHILDREN

Age Group	Boys	Girls	Total
Under 1 year	1	2	3
Between 1-5 years	2	3	5
Between 6-10 years	2	-	2
Between 11-15 years	-	2	2
16 and over	-	-	-
Total	5	7	12

Source and Method of Complaint

Source

The following table indicates the source of complaint in the 7 cases.

TABLE 17

DISTRIBUTION OF CHILD BEATING CASES ACCORDING
TO SOURCE OF COMPLAINT

Source of Complaint	Number of Families
Parents	3
Doctor	2
Landlady	1
Neighbor	1
Total	7

Juvenile police officers interviewed stated that, unlike neglect situations, complaints about beating and physical abuse of children frequently come from parents. Their observation is that while it is not uncommon for both parents to be negligent about their children, it is relatively uncommon for both parents to be cruel to their children. In this study, even though the sample of child beating and physical abuse cases is small, it tends to support this observation.

Doctors and hospitals are an important source of complaint in such cases, because the abused children often need medical attention.

Neighbors and landladies are also one of the common sources of complaints in these cases, because they are able to see and hear beating or cruelty acts of parents toward their children.

Severely beaten or abused children are seldom spotted by the police on streets or parked cars as are the neglected children. Occasionally, however, police do encounter such children when they enter a house because of complaints that parents are drunk and fighting and they may find one or more children who have signs of beating and physical cruelty.

Method

Complaints in all the seven cases were made to the police by telephone. As indicated earlier, the nature of this offense is often serious; police action is therefore immediate, irrespective of the time of day or night when complaints are received.

Investigation Procedure

The information obtained during this study indicates that, while the method of investigation of the juvenile police in abuse cases is somewhat similar to the method used in the neglect cases, their focus is quite different. As stated earlier, the police are not inclined to look for any positive elements in the family situation or take into consideration the fact that it was perhaps an isolated incident of beating caused by the father or mother who was momentarily upset or annoyed. If a child has been hurt badly, or treated cruelly by an adult, irrespective of the reason, legal action is taken.

The juvenile police involve neighbors and relatives of the family in the investigation only if they are willing; if they are, questions are asked about the child's abused condition. In cases where the child is old enough to answer questions, he is questioned about his abused condition in the presence of his parents. Similarly parents are questioned about the child's condition in the presence of the children. Juvenile police experience is that when a child has been abused by one or both parents and has received unjustifiable or cruel punishment, he seldom hesitates to admit it, even in the presence of his parents.

If the juvenile police find recent symptoms of beating and physical cruelty inflicted upon the child, these become their chief clue in conducting further investigation. In some cases, if the parents deny abusing the child, and if neighbors are unwilling or not available to give information, the juvenile police take the child to the hospital for a diagnosis of the nature and cause of the physical injury, if they think it is necessary. Illustration XXXI is an example of such a situation. Here the child was too young and the parents denied beating the child but, because she had signs of bruises on her face and body, juvenile police decided to take her to the hospital and obtain medical opinion on the nature and cause of the bruises.

Decisions

Regarding Children

Medical attention. --When physical cruelty and beating are obvious in a case, the first concern of the juvenile police is to take the child to the nearest hospital for medical attention. Colored photographs are taken of the cuts and bruises on the child's body for use as evidence. After the initial medical attention, if the doctors do not require the child to stay in the hospital, he is either taken to Juvenile Hall or returned to his parent. In the group under study, children in all 7 cases were taken to hospitals by the police for medical care. In three cases they were later admitted to Juvenile Hall.

Taking the children to the hospital, if the parents have not done so, and to Juvenile Hall or back to the parents, is the responsibility of the juvenile police officers concerned with the case. When taking children to the hospital or Juvenile Hall, the juvenile police explain to the children why and where they are being taken, and try to answer their questions and comfort them in whatever way is possible.

Filing petition. --After admitting the child or children to Juvenile Hall, a petition is filed in the juvenile court on their behalf for their care, based on facts as observed by the juvenile police, diagnosis of the doctors, testimony of the neighbors and relatives, etc. As in neglect cases, the court holds a pre-detention hearing within twenty-four hours after the petition is filed, to determine if the child should be detained in Juvenile Hall until the date of hearing or sent back to live with his parents.

In the 7 cases under study, petition was filed in 3 cases; in the remaining 4, while the adults concerned were arrested in 3 cases, the situation at home did not require the filing of petitions on behalf of the children. In 2 cases the mothers complained that the fathers had beaten the children unmercifully; so the children were returned to their mothers after receiving the necessary medical care. In one case the parents were not the offenders; a baby sitter was guilty of beating the child. In the fourth case, the child's bruises could not be diagnosed as being caused by beating.

Parents or Other Adult Offenders

Filing Criminal complaint.--A criminal complaint is filed against the adult responsible for violation of Sections 273a or 273d, or both, of the Penal Code. When, in addition to cruelty, investigating officers discover neglect or other unfit home conditions such as drunkenness and immorality, they consider the possibility of additional charges. The officers, in consultation with their supervisor, decide whether in view of the available facts the complaint should be made under more than one section of the Penal Code.

Juvenile police officers interviewed stated that whenever the situation warrants they file complaint of child beating under a felony charge. They know from experience whether the charge they are making will be supported by the evidence they have. In the group of 7 cases, complaint was filed under a felony charge in 6 cases and the adults concerned were arrested. In one case the parents were counseled and warned. When the offense is classified as a felony, the police officer can arrest the suspect immediately. This can be done because the law does not require the officer to have witnessed the commission of the offense before making an arrest for a felony charge. However, to arrest for a misdemeanor charge, police must either observe the criminal act or obtain a warrant.

Arrest.--The parents or other adults responsible in child beating cases are often arrested; however, when investigation produces little or no evidence, they are counseled and warned (Illustration XXXI). The juvenile police approach toward the adults in these cases is one of law enforcement, leading to the arrest of the offender and collection of information that will lead to his prosecution. No effort is made by the police to keep the family together as is done in some cases of neglect.

Terminating Contact with Cases

Police contact with children in these cases terminates after they have warned and counseled the parents, when the cruelty or abused condition is of a minor nature and cannot be proved. When abuse is proved, their contact terminates after arresting the offender, filing a charge of misdemeanor or felony against him, and filing a petition on behalf of the child, where necessary. In a child beating case where one parent or adult other than the child's parents is the offender, he is prosecuted but no petition is filed in the juvenile court on behalf of the child if one or both parents are able to provide a suitable home for the child.

Footnotes

[1] Vincent DeFrancis, Child Protective Services in the United States--A Nation-wide Survey (Denver: Children's Division, The American Humane Association, 1956), Chapter V.

[2]A felony is a crime which is punishable by imprisonment in the state prison; maximum penalty for a felony can be death.

[3]All units" calls are radio calls from the police headquarters alerting all police cars cruising in the city. Such calls are made in emergency situations.

[4]A misdemeanor charge is filed in the city attorney's office and the maximum punishment, if it is a jail sentence, does not exceed six months in the county jail. If it is a fine, it does not exceed $500.00. Punishment may be both a jail sentence as well as a fine. A felony charge is filed in the district attorney's office and the length of imprisonment in the state prison may not exceed five years. Maximum penalty for a felony can be death. On the basis of facts and evidence in a particular case, the city attorney or the district attorney can suggest that the case be filed with the other. Similarly, a felony charge after the preliminary trial may be reduced to a misdemeanor charge or a misdemeanor charge changed to a felony charge.

CHAPTER VI

THE ROLE OF THE JUVENILE POLICE

This study has been concerned mainly with three questions: The role of the juvenile police in the protection of neglected and abused children; the way in which the juvenile police resolve the conflicting demands of child welfare and parental punishment; and the problems encountered by the juvenile police in the absence of adequate child protective agencies. Answers to these questions, formulated in the following pages, are based on the analysis of 100 cases of neglect and abuse in the preceding chapters, supplemented by interviews with juvenile police officers who handled the cases and a review of the available literature.

As primary agents of government, responsible by law for the protection of life and property, protection of children is inherent in the very role of the police. However, as juvenile police officers their protective responsibility becomes more specific.

The overall role of the juvenile police in the area of child protection has three main phases: the receiving of complaints or detection of cases of neglected and abused children, investigation of these cases, and their disposal.

Receiving Complaints

The juvenile police services in Los Angeles City are available to the community all the twenty-four hours of the day, every day of the year. This enables the juvenile police to receive a complaint at any time of the day or night and if the situation requires, to attend to it immediately. In the group of 100 cases in this study, 64 neglect and abuse situations were brought to the attention of the police between 5:00 P.M. and 8:00 A.M. While this sample of 100 cases is too small to permit the drawing of general conclusions about the proportion of cases needing help after the normal working hours of protective and child welfare agencies, it would be fair to assume that many child neglect and abuse situations do occur at night and in some of these cases children need immediate help.

Detecting Neglected and Abused Children

The method of operation of the juvenile police and other police places them in a strategic position to spot and detect neglect cases. In the city of Los Angeles, the juvenile police cruise in the undesirable and potentially dangerous areas between the hours of 4:30 P.M. and 1:15 A.M., with the specific purpose of detecting if any juveniles are in need of help or are causing trouble. Traffic and other police units patrol all parts of the city, day and night, to enforce laws to protect the safety and rights of the general public. While doing so they come across accidents in which parents are injured and children are left uncared for; they enter homes where other crime is suspected and find neglected children; they go to arrest adults for crimes such as prostitution, shoplifting, theft, murder, and find dependent children often in a state of neglect; they check parents for drunk driving and find children sleeping in the back seat of cars. Thus they come across neglected children in many different ways because of their method of operation and through the use of the authority they have as law enforcement agents to enter homes where crime is suspected and reported. In this respect they hold a unique position in the protective program of most communities in the United States.

In the 100 cases in this study, 23 cases of neglect and abuse were detected by the juvenile and other police. This was the largest source of detection in the group when compared with other sources of complaint. These cases came to the attention of the police while they were performing their regular routine duties. When traffic and other police units come across children who are neglected or abused, they contact the juvenile police division over the two-way radio; the juvenile police, on arrival, take the necessary action to protect the children from their immediate unfit or abused condition.

Investigation

The first step in the investigation by the police is to determine whether a condition of neglect or abuse exists. If the complaint indicates that one or more children are physically hurt or are in danger of being hurt, police reach the children in the minimum possible time. However, if the complaint does not indicate any emergency, investigation begins as soon as a juvenile officer is available for the purpose. The number of juvenile police on duty during the day in the Central Division is about three times more than those on duty between 5:00 P.M. and 8:00 A.M.

On reaching the place of neglect or abuse, juvenile police, through personal observation and interviews with the complainant, neighbors, children, and parents, try to discover the nature and seriousness of the situation. Since neglecting and abusing children is a legal offense, police as law enforcement officers first have the obligation to find out if an offense against one or more children has been committed. They do this by gathering the necessary information to substantiate a possible charge.

In neglect cases they observe the physical condition of the child and the physical condition of the house. Juvenile police officers indicated that severe cases of neglect can be verified merely by observation, though they are also substantiated by information received by talking to neighbors, children, and others.

The data of this study indicate that in severe cases of neglect the children's physical condition is generally very poor. Their clothes are filthy rags, their bodies unwashed, and some children have skin rash as a result of the unclean conditions. The physical condition of the house in most cases of severe neglect is extremely filthy, with dirty clothes and dishes all over the house, filthy and clogged toilets, unpleasant odors, and generally unkempt conditions throughout. In some cases broken bottles, knives, and tin cans lie on the floor, while the children run around without any shoes. Juvenile police frequently take pictures when they find the physical condition of the house very bad; this is done to provide evidence in the court in contested cases.

The less severe cases of neglect, however, need more detailed investigation because the exact nature of the neglect is often not obvious. In these cases the juvenile police, by talking to the complainant, neighbors, children, and parents, if they are available, gather information to discover the seriousness of the neglect condition to learn whether it is a chronic condition of neglect or an isolated incident.

Investigation procedure in the abuse cases differs in some ways, depending upon the nature of the abused condition. The 30 cases of abuse in this study fell in two categories: the sexual abuse of children and child beating.

In sexual abuse cases, investigation starts with what the child victim is able to tell the juvenile police about the nature of the abuse. This is supplemented, where necessary, with medical examination reports. Juvenile police stated, and the sample in the study substantiated, that in this category of cases the majority are minor sexual molestations of young children by men. Frequently such molestation does not result in physical injury. However, investigation of these cases becomes complex when the child is below five years of age. Often, such young children are unable to recall the details of the incident accurately or describe the offender adequately. If the juvenile police are not able to gather these facts, it becomes difficult for them to locate the offender or to file a criminal complaint against him.[1] It is also necessary in some cases that the child should be able to give the facts accurately in the City/District Attorney's office, so that a criminal complaint against the offender may be filed and accepted.

Officers interviewed for this study stated that in some cases of sexual abuse no action can be taken for lack of evidence, because the victims are too young to give an accurate account in the City/District Attorney's office.

They further stated that it is not uncommon for them to come across case of minor sexual abuse where the parents are unwilling to allow the child to describe the incident to the juvenile police or go to the court to testify. Such parents are generally concerned about the traumatic and unpleasant experience which their child has had and do not want him to go over it again. In such situations juvenile police have no choice but to close the case without taking any action.

Investigation of child beating cases does not present the same problems as the sexual abuse cases. In most cases of child beating, there is visible proof of abuse.

However, to substantiate the evidence, the child victim, his parents, neighbor, and the complainant are interviewed. The child is taken to the nearest hospital for a medical examination and treatment if necessary, and colored photographs are taken in case of severe beating. The medical report and the colored photographs form a part of the investigation report of the juvenile police.

Disposal

The disposal of any case of child neglect or abuse depends upon the facts and evidence obtained during investigation. The primary responsibility of the juvenile police as law enforcement officers is to find, through investigation, whether the parents or adults in any situation of neglect and abuse have physically harmed a child, endangered his health or life, or have treated him cruelly. If so, legal action on the part of the police is mandatory. However, if investigation shows that, while a law is broken, the child has not been harmed, juvenile officers in consultation with their supervisors decide their line of action, weighing the positive and negative factors in the case. These cases are know as "grey" situations, and law may or may not be enforced. Discretion is a part of law enforcement and judgment is used by juvenile officers in the "grey" situations of neglect in deciding whether legal action is necessary.

According to the existing child protection laws in California, dependency and unfit home conditions resulting in the physical and moral neglect of a child are handled under Sections 700b and 700d of the Welfare and Institutions Code, which focuses its concern on the welfare of the child. However, neglect in which the parents or any other adult's negligence has endangered the life or health of the child, physical abuse resulting in severe and unjustifiable beating, and sexual abuse of various types are handled under the various sections of the Penal Code, which aims at punitive retribution of crime (Appendix A).

Analysis of cases in this study and interviews with juvenile police officers indicate that in most cases of neglect the following factors help the juvenile police to decide that they can operate under the various sections of the Welfare and Institutions Code:

1.   When children in a family are neglected due to the physical or mental ill health of the parents. In such cases the parents are unable to care for their children owing to conditions beyond their control. Most such cases are booked by the juvenile police under Section 700b of the Welfare and Institutions Code and these children are classed as "dependent" children. The juvenile court is requested to make arrangement for their placement until the parents are well and able to re-assume their responsibilities.

2.   When one or both parents are found to be leaving their children without any adult care for long periods of time during the day or night. Sometimes the neglect is confined only to this condition; the children are otherwise taken care of adequately and the parents show willingness to improve the situation. Such cases are booked under Section 700b and the children are left with the parents who are "counseled and warned" about

the legal consequence of neglecting their children. In such cases the juvenile police tell these parents that they will pay a surprise visit to see if they have improved the condition of the children and the house. Visits are paid if the police have any cause to doubt the parents' ability to improve as promised.

3. When the neglect condition of children is of a minor nature, an isolated or unintentional incident, the case is booked under Section 700b of the Welfare and Institutions Code. Cases of lost children are booked under this section and the children are usually released to the parents as soon as they are located.

4. When neglect conditions even of a minor nature are associated with parents' drinking in the presence of their children, the cases are booked under Section 700d of the Welfare and Institutions Code. These are classed as "unfit" homes and juvenile police take legal action. Other crimes frequently found associated with "unfit homes" are prostitution, gambling, thieving, and the like. If parents are found in an intoxicated condition when the juvenile police reach the house, they are arrested for becoming intoxicated in the presence of children; their children are taken to Juvenile Hall unless a relative or a neighbor volunteers to care for them. However, children are not left with relatives or neighbors when police find that the parents' drunkenness and the children's neglect are chronic conditions. In such cases, they arrest the parents and remove the children to Juvenile Hall. A petition is filed in the juvenile court the following day on behalf of the children, stating that the parents through their negligence and depravity in forms such as prostitution, gambling, thieving, drunkenness, are providing an "unfit" home for the children.

Thus, within the provisions of the Welfare and Institutions Code, juvenile police book the neglect cases of less serious nature under Section 700b and those indicating a chronic condition of neglect associated with depraved living conditions under Section 700d.

The juvenile police work under the Penal Code when the following conditions are associated with neglect and abuse cases:

1. If in a neglect case parental negligence or negligence of other adults, drunkenness, and other habits have endangered the lives or health of the children in any way, the case is booked under Section 273a of the Penal Code. As stated earlier, in the severe neglect cases the house is often extremely filthy and unhygienic and children are underclothed and underfed and left uncared for. This is an indication of parental negligence resulting in the possibility of endangering the life and health of children.

2. A single act of neglect may sometimes be booked under Section 273a if it is serious and has endangered the life or health of the child. An example is Illustration XIV in Chapter IV.[2]

3. Cases of child beating are booked under Section 273d of the Penal Code. In these cases the beating has resulted in severe bruises or lacerations. A "spanking" of the child by parents which produces discoloration of the skin is not considered violation of this section. However, once the fact of severe beating is established in a case, the parent or adult responsible for it is arrested. Child beating is an act of "commission"

and is punishable as a felony. If beating also results in endangering the life or limb of the child, juvenile police book the case under Section 273d as well as Section 273a of the Penal Code. In most child beating cases the line of action of the police is set. They do not take the child to Juvenile Hall unless the child has only one parent, who is being prosecuted. If there are two parents and only one is guilty and being prosecuted, the child is left in his own home.

A felony charge is filed against the offending parent with the office of the District Attorney. Juvenile officers know from experience if the evidence they have will support the charge they make in a case. If the physical cruelty is not too severe and has not resulted in broken bones or other injuries but is severe enough to be considered a violation of law, a misdemeanor complaint is filed with the City Attorney's office.

4.   All cases of sexual abuse of children are booked under various sections of the Penal Code. No sexual abuse case is booked under the Welfare and Institutions Code. Juvenile police stated, and the data substantiated, that Sections 288 and 647a(1) of the Penal Code of California cover sexual crimes most frequently committed by adults against children.

Sexual crimes such as homosexual activities of older men with young boys and molestation of young girls by men are booked under Section 288 of the Penal Code, which is punishable as a felony. Cases of "mild annoyance" of young boys or girls are booked under Section 647a(i) of the Penal Code, which is punishable as a misdemeanor if it is a first offense, and as a felony if the offender has a prior conviction under this section.

Neglect cases initially booked under Section 700b may be changed to Section 700d, if investigation reveals that neglect conditions are chronic and more severe than they appeared to be before all the facts were available. Similarly, cases initially booked under Section 700d of the Welfare and Institutions Code may be changed to Section 273a of the Penal Code if investigation shows that parents have endangered the children's life and health. However, when a neglect condition is found to be chronic or severe, legal action by juvenile police is mandatory.

Thus, within the provisions of the Penal Code, juvenile police provide protection to children from adult negligence and abuse endangering their life or health, physical abuse or cruelty such as beating and other cruel acts, and sexual abuses of various kinds.

Causes of Child Neglect and Abuse

As viewed by the Juvenile Police

Interviews with twelve juvenile police officers who handled the cases in this study indicated that they have a sympathetic understanding of the reasons why parents neglect their children and do not consider these parents to be mere "offenders" who deserve nothing but "punishment." All twelve officers expressed belief that there is always a combination of reasons why parents neglect and abuse their children. These were enumerated as immaturity and selfishness in parents, unstable income, and marital disharmony. Excessive drinking was observed by all respondents to be associated with over 50 percent of the cases of neglect which they handle. Six officers were of the opinion that some parents neglect their children because they do not know any better. These parents tend to provide the same pattern of life for their children as was provided them by their parents.

As viewed by Social Welfare Agencies

Social welfare agencies view the parental neglect and abuse of children as a serious personal and social problem and believe that "the parent who finds so little satisfaction in one of the most deeply personal relationships that living provides has surely suffered a long series of mishaps that make him the fearful, immature, unstable person that he is . . ."[3]

Social workers prominent in the field of child welfare in this country believe that emotional problems in the parents are a major cause of child neglect and abuse. Frequently the cause of these problems can be traced back to deprivation and unhappiness in the parents' own childhood.[4] It is therefore important for protective and child welfare agencies to help these parents, through casework service, to come to grips with the problems which cause them to neglect and abuse their children. Child protective services are defined as a "specialized casework service to neglected, abused, exploited or rejected children. The focus of the service is preventive and non-punitive and is geared toward a rehabilitation of the home and a treatment of the motivating factors which underlie neglect . . ."[5] Such a service, in most cases of child neglect and abuse, is on an "involuntary" basis because parents who neglect or abuse their children seldom seek help voluntarily.

Common Goal with Different Roles

It is obvious that both the police and the child welfare agencies have a common goal with regard to the neglected and abused children. It is protection of children from neglect and abuse. However, the roles of the two agencies are quite different.

The police as law enforcement officers have responsibility of removing a child from a neglect or abuse situation; they are equipped to do this twenty-four hours of the day and every day of the year because they never cease vigilance. The method of operation and the legal authority which police have to enter homes where crime is suspected puts them in a strategic position, on the first line of defense, to protect the neglected and abused child from its immediate unfit situation.

The protective and other child welfare agencies, on the other hand, are not equipped to detect neglected and abused children in the way police are. Thus, the police supplement the child welfare services by being able to detect and protect these children in many different ways at all times. However, while the focus of the child welfare agencies in this area is on rehabilitating the home and keeping the family together where possible, the juvenile police, being primarily a law enforcement agency, are obliged to take legal action when the situation so requires. The police are neither equipped nor do they attempt to rehabilitate a home. They avoid removing the neglected or abused children from their homes if they can, but, as the analysis of the cases shows, this is not always possible.

The juvenile police officers interviewed showed awareness of the need for protective and child welfare agencies in the community, recognizing the fact that law enforcement and child welfare agencies have separate roles in the protection of the neglected and abused children, and that neither is equpped to substitute for the other. This fact is also generally recognized and is being emphsized by leaders in the law enforcement field. In a paper presented by Lt. M. R. Hibbard, Juvenile Control Officer in the State of Washinton, at the 1960 Utah Welfare Meeting (where he was representing the International Juvenile Police Officers Assocation), he stated:

> The mark of a good juvenile officer is to know his limitations. This also applies to departments as well. The good officer must know what he is not. He is not a probation officer, he is not a recreational expert, and he is not a social worker. However, he should be aware of what agencies in the community can provide these services and he should be wise enough to see that a child in need of these services is referred to the proper agency.[6]

Lynn D. Swanson, Consultant on Police Services in the U. S. Children's Bureau, Department of Health, Education, and Welfare, brings out a similar point in one of his papers.

> Another problem area is the involvement of police in probation services. This usually involves supervision of a child on a continuing basis, for a definite or indefinite period. It is likened to a casework treatment service by social agencies. Again, as in the case of recreation programs, police are not trained for this type of service. Moreover, other agencies have been given the responsibility for providing these services.[7]

Similarly, a social worker or a child welfare worker is not a law enforcement officer and is therefore not in the same strategic position and does not have the same facilities as a law enforcement officer to detect neglect and abuse conditions. However, by supplementing each other's services, many more neglected children and their parents could be helped.

Absence of Adequate Protective Services

The joint effort, however, is only possible when, along with law enforcement, adequate protective and child welfare services also exist in a community. This is unfortunately not always so, and many communities in the United States do not have adequate child welfare services to meet the needs of their neglected and abused children; Los Angeles, with its fast growing population, is one of them.[8] The lack of adequate protective services handicaps the efforts of the juvenile police in protecting the neglected and abused children.

Juvenile officers interviewed for this study believed that at least some of the parents who neglect their children need help other than just "punishment," which is often all they receive at present. The Probation Department of Los Angeles, like most probation departments, has a large case load to handle. The result is that in many cases of neglect, parents who are released by the court on probation do not receive enough casework service; as a result, they come back to the attention of juvenile police a second or even a third time. The juvenile police were of the opinion that the less severe cases of neglect need more than mere counseling and warning. In this study, 40 percent of the neglect cases were terminated by the police with counseling and warning. Here is where they definitely recognized the need for protective agencies to which these cases could be referred. Their experience is that, due to the limited amount of such services in this community, the minor neglect cases are overlooked for a while by them until they become more serious cases, and then the police are obliged to take legal action. Though no figures can be quoted, all the officers interviewed expressed belief that in their experience some minor neglect cases have become serious cases because no help could be given to them when their problem was of a less serious nature. In some chronic cases of neglect, where the neglect may not be of a serious nature but exists for some time, police are obliged to take legal action mainly because there are not enough agencies in the community equipped to handle such cases. As law enforcement officers, they cannot overlook a neglect situation.

The second problem which the police face because of the lack of protective agencies, is the temporary placement of children. The majority of the children, in minor as well as serious cases of neglect, have to be admitted to Juvenile Hall, which is frequently overcrowded. The foster homes facilities for such children, developed by the Bureau of Public Assistance, are very limited. In some minor neglect cases the children have to be removed from their homes for a few hours only because the juvenile police are not able to leave young children by themselves in the absence of their parents. Adequate protective services would enable such children to remain in their home with the help of a worker until some arrangement is made for them.

Lack of Mutual Understanding

It is unfortunate that police and social welfare agencies are so often in a state of coexistence rather than cooperation, in the field of child protection. This may be because neither has made enough effort to understand the philosophy, functions, and limits of the other, even though they both have the same objective--protection of children. To quote Lt. M. R. Hibbard again:

> Although there have been some experiments leading to closer cooperation between the social agencies and law enforcement agencies, there is much more that could be done along these lines . . . I think that every community needs some sort of forum or meeting place where law enforcement and social agencies (and I wish to include the school representatives also) should regularly sit down together to discuss better ways of getting at our growing delinquency and other problems related to children. Maybe we do have different philosophies and maybe we do speak a different language, but

maybe if we got together, often enough, we might find outselves learning from each other and if we ever do that, we may be surprised to find that we like each other. [9]

The social work profession must shoulder its part of the blame for having done little to understand the vital role of the police, in a program which is the common concern of both professions. The old association of child protection with law enforcement, which is responsible to a great extent for the existing lack of cooperation, should not be allowed to remain a barrier in the future. Protection of children in any community is a total community problem and is not the sole responsibility of any one agency.

Interviews with juvenile officers revealed two significant points with reference to the social work profession.

Five out of the twelve officers interviewed had questions about the effectiveness of the child welfare and other social welfare agencies in helping families who neglect or abuse their children. (This was mainly based on their experience with one or more welfare agencies in the community.) In their opinion these agencies tend to have a very "Lenient" approach which is ineffective in bringing about the desired change in parents. However, most of the officers expressed the opinion that, because of their limited and brief contacts with such agencies, their understanding of the policies and method of work of welfare agencies was also limited.

Eight out of the twelve juvenile officers expressed the opinion that welfare agencies are critical of police methods of handling neglected children. (This was again based on their individual experiences.) They believe that these agencies are of the opinion that juvenile police are purely legalistic in their approach and, therefore, are concerned mainly with "punishing the offender." As one of the officers put it, "they forget that we are human beings first and police officers next;" however, since law enforcement is their primary responsibility, it must be carried out where necessary.

Some Suggestions for Closer Cooperation and Better Coordination

Closer cooperation between the juvenile police and Social Welfare agencies is of great importance and can be achieved only if each understands the other's philosophy, function, and limits. There are various ways by which such cooperation can be obtained.

One way to make this possible is for Social Welfare agencies interested in the protection of children to take the lead, by inviting juvenile police officers to their staff meetings for consideration of common problems and goals. This would give the juvenile police an opportunity to know that they are not only an important part of the team but that their role is vital in the protection of the children. Once understanding and acceptance of each other's role is established, several other possibilities may develop to help each other work more effectively.

Another possibility which the juvenile police units can explore is that of using the services of social workers in their units, particularly in the investigation of neglect and abuse cases. Such an arrangement would help the juvenile police in their decision about certain cases that might not need to be taken to the court. This decision is not always positive and possible when police officers operate under their usual work pressures, limited time, and within the framework of law enforcement.

In a recent article Mr. Swanson point out that:

> While it is generally recognized that police departments have an important function in protecting children who are neglected in most communities, no agreement has been reached by either police departments or community agencies as to the appropriate role of the police. Nor has there been effective coordination of police activities of other agencies.[10]

Lack of coordination seems to be a major problem which the two agencies face today in many communities. However, a few communities have overcome this problem to some extent by coordinating their services and shouldering the responsibility of child protection jointly.

The Protective Services Unit of the City and County Department of Welfare, Denver, Colorado, is apparently an example of such coordination.[11] This unit, in cooperation with the police, receives all telephone calls regarding complaints of neglect or abuse during the daytime hours, including those which are made to the police department. A social worker for the unit makes the initial visit and if children are found to be in danger and immediate removal is necessary, she refers the matter to the Juvenile Bureau officer. He then initiates action on behalf of the child but refers the parent to the protective services for planning. However, during the night hours, the district police officers respond to any emergency calls regarding neglected or abused children and take necessary action. The following morning, Juvenile Bureau officers in cooperation with the district police officers, take whatever subsequent police action is necessary and simultaneously refer the parents to the Protective Services Unit. For effective coordination, the Juvenile Bureau officers and the Protective Unit worker confer daily regarding individual complaints and where necessary plan jointly regarding the best way to handle a complaint.

This seems to be a good example of a coordinated program where each agency supplements the other's work. Where possible, more communities should experiment with similar plans of coordination. In the city of Los Angeles, each geographic police division has a juvenile division, and such a plan could function very effectively.

Conclusions

The role of the juvenile police in the protection of neglected and abused children in one area of the city of Los Angeles has been examined in this study. It is the researcher's opinion that, within the framework of law enforcement, the juvenile police are providing the children of this area the best possible protection which their resources permit. The law is enforced with discretion where humane consideration and judgment call for welfare services rather than parental punishment. However, the best possible protection for its neglected and abused children can be provided by a community only when both law enforcement and welfare services are adequate; each has a distinct role and neither can substitute for the other.

The experimental Protective Service Unit of the Bureau of Public Assistance in Los Angeles appears to be a step in the right direction. It is to be hoped that this experiment will lead to the establishment of more child protective services which, in cooperation with the juvenile police, will be able to offer better and more effective protection to the neglected and abused children.

Footnotes

[1] The 16 cases of abuse marked as "no action" cases, and deleted from this study, were in this category.

[2] Here, the mother had locked her three month infant in a car for over two hours while she was drinking in a bar with another of her children. Juvenile police did not know how often the mother did this and the case was not investigated any further. However, the facts of the one incident indicated that the mother had endangered the life of the baby. He could have died from heat exhaustion.

[3] Claire R. Hancock, "Protective Services for Children," Child Welfare, March 1949, p. 4.

[4] John Bowlby, Maternal Care and Mental Health, A report prepared on behalf of the World Health Organization as a contribution to the United Nations Program for the Welfare of Homeless Children (Geneva: World Health Organization, 1952), p. 78.

[5] Vincent DeFrancis, Child Protective Services in the United States--A Nation-wide Survey (Denver: Children's Division, The American Humane Association, 1956), p. 18.

[6] Lt. M. R. Hibbard, "Working to Curtail Crime and Delinquency" (unpublished paper read at the Utah Welfare Meeting, Salt Lake, December 1960), p. 3.

[7] Lynn D. Swanson, "Police and Children--Total Police Specialization to Children is Not Feasible," The Police Chief (June 1958), p. 22.

[8] Welfare Planning Council, Los Angeles Region, A Protective Service Program (Los Angeles: Welfare Planning Council, 1956), p. 3.

[9] Hibbard, op. cit., p. 3.

[10]Lynn D. Swanson, "Role of the Police in the Protection of Children from Neglect and Abuse," _Federal Probation,_ March 1961, p. 43.

[11]American Public Welfare Association, "Preventive and Protective Services to Children, a Responsibility of the Public Welfare Agency" (Summary of material presented by participants in an institute sponsored by the American Public Welfare Association, Chicago, March 1958), pp. 13-15.

APPENDIX A

SECTIONS OF THE WELFARE AND INSTITUTIONS CODE AND THE PENAL CODE

OF THE STATE OF CALIFORNIA FOR THE PROTECTION OF

NEGLECTED AND ABUSED CHILDREN

WELFARE AND INSTITUTIONS CODE AND LAWS RELATIVE TO SOCIAL
WELFARE STATE OF CALIFORNIA - 1957

Article 6 - Jurisdiction of the Juvenile Court

700 - The jurisdiction of the juvenile court extends to any person under the age of 21 years who comes within any of the following descriptions:

(a) Who is found begging, receiving or gathering alms or who is found in any street, road or public place for the purpose of so doing whether actually begging or doing so under the pretext of selling or offering for sale any article or of singing or playing on any musical instrument or of giving any public entertainment or accompanying or being used in aid of any person so doing.

(b) Who has no parent or guardian, or who has no parent or guardian willing to exercise or capable of exercising proper parental control and who is in need of such control.

(c) Who is a destitute or who is not provided with the necessities of life by his parents and who has no other means of obtaining such necessities.

(d) Whose home is an unfit place for him by reason of neglect, cruelty or depravity of either of his parents, or of his guardian or other person in whose custody or care he is.

(e) Who is found wandering and either has no home, no settled place of abode, no visible means of subsistence or no proper guardianship.

Section

702 - Any person who commits any act or omits the performance of any duty which act or ommission causes or tends to cause or encourage any person under the age of 21 years to come within the provisions of any of the subdivisions of Section 700 . . . is guilty of a misdemeanor and upon conviction thereof shall be punished by a fine not exceeding one thousand dollars or by imprisonment in the county jail for not more than one year or by both such fine and imprisonment in a county jail or may be released on probation for a period not exceeding five years.

Jurisdiction of court:

The juvenile court shall have original jurisdiction over all misdemeanors defined in this section . . .

(Laws relating to the protection of abused children, applicable
in the State of California in 1958)

§ 261 - Rape defined

Rape is an act of sexual intercourse, accomplished with a female not the wife of the perpetrator, under either of the following circumstances:

1. Where the female is under the age of eighteen years;

2. Where she is incapable, through lunacy or other unsoundness of mind, whether temporary or permanent, of giving legal consent;

3. Where she resists, but her resistence is overcome by force or violence;

4. Where she is prevented from resisting by threats of great and immediate bodily harm, accompanied by apparent power of execution, or by any intoxicating narcotic, or anesthetic substance, administered by or with the privity of the accused;

5. Where she is at the time unconscious of the nature of the act, and this is known to the accused;

6. Where she submits under the belief that the person committing the act is her husband and this belief is induced by any artifice, pretence, or concealment practiced by the accused, with intent to induce such belief.

§273a Wilful cruelty toward child: Endangering health or life

Any person who wilfully causes or permits any child to suffer or who inflicts thereon unjustifiable physical pain or mental suffering, and whoever, having the care or custody of any child, causes or permits the life or limb of such child to be injured, is guilty of a misdemeanor.

§273d Infliction of traumatic injury upon wife or child

Any husband who wilfully inflicts upon his wife corporal injury resulting in a traumatic condition, and any person who wilfully inflicts upon any child any cruel or inhuman corporal punishment or injury resulting in a traumatic condition is guilty of a felony and upon conviction, thereof, shall be punished by imprisonment in a state prison for not more than two years or in the county jail for not more than one year.

§273g Immoral practices or habitual drunkenness in presence of children

Any person who in the presence of any child indulges in any degrading, lewd, immoral or vicious habits or practices or who is habitually drunk in the presence of any child in his care, custody or control, is guilty of a misdemeanor.

§285 Incest defined: Punishment

Persons being within the degree of consanguinity within which marriages are declared by law to be incestuous and void, who intermarry with each other or who commit fornication or adultery with each other are punishable by imprisonment in the state prison not less than one year nor more than fifty years.

§288 Crimes against children: Lewd and lascivious acts: Punishment

Any person who shall wilfully and lewdly commit any lewd or lascivious act including any of the acts constituting other crimes provided for in part one of this code, upon or with the body, or any part or member thereof, of a child under the age of fourteen years, with the intent of arousing appealing to, or gratifying the lust or passions or sexual desires of such person or of such child, shall be guilty of a felony and shall be imprisoned in the state prison for a term of from one year to life.

§311 Indecent exposures, exhibitions, etc.:

. . . exposes his person, or the private parts thereof in any public place, or in any place where there are present other persons to be offended or annoyed thereby . . . is guilty of a misdemeanor.

§647a Annoying children or loitering where school children attend

(1)   Every person who annoys or molests any child is a vagrant and is punishable upon first conviction by a fine of not exceeding five hundred dollars or by imprisonment in the county jail for not exceeding six months or by both such fine and imprisonment and is punishable upon the second and each subsequent conviction by imprisonment in the state prison not exceeding five years.

(2)   Every person who loiters about any school or public place at or near which school children attend is a vagrant and is punishable by a fine of not exceeding five hundred dollars or by imprisonment in the county jail for not exceeding six months or by both such fine and imprisonment.

APPENDIX B

SCHEDULE

ANALYSES OF JUVENILE RECORDS

IDENTIFYING INFORMATION:

       Case Number   Date

1.   Name of Child/Children   Age   Sex   Racial Origin

2.   Name of Parents or Guardians   Age

3.   Home address

4.   Occupation

5.   Complaint

6.   Original Charge

7.   Final Charge

8.   Disposition of the Case

9.   Investigating Officer

10.   Prior record of neglect: Yes_____, No_____, When_____

11.   What was the disposition then

12.   Was petition filed under the present complaint? Yes_____, No_____

COMPLAINT

1.   Who made the complaint?

2.   How was it made, by phone____, by letter____, in person____

3.   When was it made?

INVESTIGATION

1. When did the investigation start?

2. Who was contacted first?

3. Who else was contacted besides the parents? School____, Neighbor____, Relatives____, Others____

4. How was evidence of abuse or neglect established?

5. In case of missing parents, were neighbors contacted?

6. Was the child questioned? Yes____, No____
   What kind of questions was he asked?

7. What was his reaction? Frightened____, Confused____, Indifferent____, Upset____, Other____

8. If parents were present, what were their reactions to investigation?

9. Did they cooperate with the police?

DECISION MAKING

1. What decision was made?

2. Why was this particular decision made?

3. Could you have made an alternate decision in this case? Why/Why not?
   Did your supervisor agree to the decision?

4. Parents' reactions to the decision.

5. Children's reactions to the decision? Cried____, Became fearful____, Took it as a matter of fact____, Other____.

6. How was decision conveyed to the children?

7. If this was possible, what specific attempts were made to keep the family together?

EXECUTIION OF DECISION

1. What happened to the parents? a. arrested____, b. warned____, asked to contact police____, referred to a welfare agency____, other____.

2. What happened to the child/children?

   a. taken to Juvenile Hall____ some other institution____
   b. left with the parents____
   c. left with neighbors____
   d. left with relatives____
   e. removed to the hospital____
   f. any other.

3.   If removed to Juvenile Hall, what were they told about it?

4.   How did they react to it?

5.   Was any preparation made for their removal to Juvenile Hall?

6.   Who accompanied them there?

7.   Police activities at Juvenile Hall.

8.   Was any further investigation made before filing the petition?

9.   Was your presence necessary at the pre-detention hearings. If so, why?

10.   Did you attend the hearing to testify?

11.   At what point was contact terminated with the case?

GENERAL QUESTIONS

1.   What is your opinion about this case?

2.   Do you think it was a chronic or isolated case of abuse and/or neglect. Why?

3.   Why do you think parents neglect and abuse their children?

4.   Is the present arrangement of dealing with the problem of neglect satisfactory? If not, why not?

5.   What do you think is the police role in the protective program of this community?

6.   Which are the welfare agencies in this community where you refer cases of mild neglect?

7.   Do you keep in touch with them or they with you, about the case referred?

8.   Any other comments.

APPENDIX C

INSTRUCTION SHEET USED AS A REFERENCE BY JUVENILE POLICE

WHEN HANDLING CASES OF CHILD NEGLECT AND ABUSE

I.   GENERAL

    A.   Juvenile defined

        1.   Person under the age of 18 years.

    B.   Minor defined

        1.   Person under the age of 21 years.

    C.   Juvenile Court

        1.   Has exclusive jurisdiction over persons under 18 years of age. Case must be referred to Juvenile Court first (825 W. I. C.)

        2.   Has concurrent jurisdiction with regular courts over persons from 18 to 20 years inclusive.

        3.   Brought before Juvenile Court by Petition or by Certification from another court.

        4.   If detained, petition must be presented to Juvenile Court within two court days.

        5.   Purpose of Juvenile Court action to declare subject ward of court.

        6.   Court may allow probation and release or placement, may admonish and dismiss, place with California Youth Authority.

        7.   Proceeding not a conviction, subject not in jeopardy.

II. WELFARE AND INSTITUTIONS CODE

    A.   Section 700. The jurisdiction of the Juvenile Court extends to all minors who come within one of the following subsections:

        a.   Begging, receiving or gathering alms.

b. Applies to juveniles who have no parent or guardian; **or** who has no parent or guardian willing to exercise or capable of exercising proper parental control; or who has no parent or guardian actually exercizing such proper parental control and who is in need of such control.

c. Destitute, not provided with necessities of life by parents.

d. This section is used to book dependent children. It would appear on the booking slip as 700D WIC (Unfit home) Dep. This section is used to take children into protective custody where one or both of the parents or his guardians, because of neglect, cruelty, or depravity, maintain an unfit home for the child. It will be noted that a child is a dependent in this case and not a delinquent.

B. Section 702 (Contributing to the Delinquency of Minor)

Any person who commits any act or omits to perform duty which causes or tends to cause any minor to come within the provisions of one of the subsections of Section 700 is guilty of Contributing to the Delinquency of a Minor. For example, if an adult person encourages or leads a juvenile female to become sexually promiscuous, then he would violate this section.

III. PENAL CODE

A. Section 647a.1 P.C. (Annoying or Molesting Child)

ELEMENTS:

1. Every person who annoys or molests a child under 18 years (whether attending school or not).

   It is a misdemeanor - (Example) - A person who makes a lewd advance or lewd and obscene language, tries to get young child into car.

   Molestation should be of sexual nature.

   Person who has prior conviction of this section or prior conviction of 288 P.C. and violates this section commits a felony.

B. Section 647a.2 P.C. (Loitering Near School)

It is a misdemeanor for any person, age not element, to loiter around any school or public place at or near which school children attend.

This section was apparently passed to keep possible sex offenders from loitering around places where children attend. Violation is a misdemeanor. Used to prevent loitering by kids not attending, or attending at other school.

C. Section 311.1 P.C. (Indecent Exposure)

ELEMENTS:

1. Expose person or private parts in any public place or any place

where there are present other persons to be offended or annoyed thereby. (Misdemeanor) This is probably the most common of all sex offenses against children.

One who commits this offense and has a prior conviction for indecent exposure or of 288 P.C. has committed a felony.

The Juvenile Division is responsible for the investigation of all indecent exposure whether the victim is a juvenile or adult.

D.   Section 285 P.C. (Incest)

ELEMENTS:

1.   Persons within the degrees of consanguinity, marries or engages in sexual intercourse:

   A.   Child and parents
   B.   Ancestors and descendants
   C.   Brother and sister (whole or half)
   D.   Uncles and nieces
   E.   Nephews and aunts

   Punishable as a felony.

E.   Section 288 P.C (Crime Against Child)

ELEMENTS:

1.   Any person who wilfully and lewdly commits any lewd or lascivious acts, upon or with the body or any part of the body, of a child under the age of fourteen years with the intent of arousing, appealing to, or gratifying the lust or passions or sexual desires of himself or the child is guilty of a felony. It is not necessary to touch the naked body. If killing occurs during 288 P.C., First Degree Murder.

F.   Section 261.1 P.C. (Statutory Rape)

ELEMENTS:

1.   Sexual intercourse with female not wife of perpetrator, and she is under age of 18 years.

2.   Consent of the victim is no defense, even if female shows what purports to be proof of age.

3.   For arrest purposes violation of this section is a felony; however, court or jury trying same can prescribe a county jail sentence.

G.   Section 273a P.C. (Endangering Life, Limb of Child)

ELEMENTS:

1.   Inflict unjustifiable pain or mental suffering. Or, permits life or limb of child to be in danger, or health of child to be injured.

Punishable as a misdemeanor.

Used in cases where there are very unsanitary home conditions, dirt, filth, rotten food, or when parents get into a drunken battle and throw things at one another in child's presence, very drunk on street with small child.

Advisable for officers to arrange for photos to be taken of scene for evidentiary purposes.

H.   Section 273d P. C.   (Child Beating)

This is the same section that is used for wife-beating.

ELEMENTS:

1.   Any person who wilfully inflicts cruel punishment resulting in traumatic injury on person of child.   (In wife beating, offender must be husband; in child beating, offender may be any person.)

For practical purposes and for prosecution under this section, traumatic injury must consist of some severe bruise or laceration, A mere spanking of child by father which produces discolorations of the skin would not be a violation of this section.   The injuries inflicted and the cause therefor would have to be unreasonable.

Violation is a felony.   Photos of the child should be taken for evidentiary purposes.

I.   Section 273g P. C. (Immoral Practices in Presence of Children)

ELEMENTS:

1.   Immoral habits or practices in presence of child.   Habitual intoxication in presence of child.   Any child in care, custody, control, not necessarily own child.

Commission of a single act of an immoral nature or intoxication would be insufficient under this section.   A habitual pattern would have to be proved.

Violation is a misdemeanor.

IV.   MUNICIPAL CODE

A.   Section 45.03A LAMC (Curfew)

ELEMENTS:

1.   Child under age of 18 years.

Loiter on any public street or any public place between 10 p.m. and sunrise without parent or guardian or spouse over 21.

Essential element is loitering.

Subsection B of this ordinance makes it a misdemeanor for any parent or guardian to allow or permit their child to violate the curfew ordinance.

BIBLIOGRAPHY

Books

Abbott, Grace. The Child and the State. Chicago: The University of Chicago Press, 1938. Vols. I and II.

Black, Henry Campbell. Black's Law Dictionary. Minnesota: West Publishing Co., 1951.

Bowen, Loise De Koven. Safeguards for City Youth, at Work and at Play. New York: The Macmillan Company, 1914.

Bowerman, E. E. The Laws of Child Protection. London: Sir Isaac Pitman and Sons, and Sons, Ltd., 1933.

Bowlby, J. Maternal Care and Mental Health. Geneva, Switzerland: World Health Organization, 1955.

California, State of. Welfare and Institutions Code and Laws Relating to Social Welfare. Sacramento: Documents Section, Printing Division, 1957.

Cameron, Norman. The Psychology of Behavior Disorders. Boston: Houghton Mifflin Company, 1947.

Chesser, Eustace. Cruelty to Children. New York: Philosophical Library, Inc., 1952.

Davis, Kingsley. Human Society. New York: The Macmillan Company, 1949.

De Francis, Vincent. Child Protective Services in the United States: A Nationwide Survey. Denver: Children's Division, The American Humane Association, 1956.

_____. The Fundamentals of Child Protection. Denver: Children's Division, The American Humane Association, 1955.

Deering's Penal Code of the State of California. San Francisco: Bancroft-Whitney Company, 1949.

Folks, Homer. The Care of Destitute, Neglected and Delinquent Children. New York: The Macmillan Co., 1911.

Fuller, Edward. The Right of the Child. Boston: The Beacon Press, 1951.

Glueck, Sheldon and Eleanor. Delinquents in the Making: Paths to Prevention. New York: Harper and Brothers, 1952.

Gross, N., and W. S. Mason and A. W. McEachern. Explorations in Role Analysis. New York: John Wiley and Sons, Inc., 1958.

Hamilton, Mary E. The Policewoman, Her Services and Ideals. New York: Frederick A Stokes Company, 1926.

Kenney, John P., and Dan Pursuit. Police Work with Juveniles. Illinois: Charles C. Thomas Publishers, 1954.

Linton, Ralph. The Study of Man. New York: Appleton-Century Co., 1936.

_____. The Cultural Background of Personality. New York: Appleton-Century Co., 1945.

Lundberg, Emma O. Unto the Least of These. New York: D. Appleton-Century Company, 1947.

McCrea, Roswell C. The Humane Movement. New York: Columbia University Press, 1910.

Murphy, Gardner. Personality--A Biosocial Approach to Origins and Structure. New York: Harper and Brothers, 1947.

Newcomb, Theodore M. Social Psychology. New York: The Dryden Press, 1950.

Owings, Chloe. Women Police--A Study of the Development and Status of Women Police Movement. New York: Frederick H. Hitchcock, 1925.

Parsens, Talcott. Essays in Sociological Theory. Illinois: The Free Press, 1954.

Pigeon, Helen D., and others. Principles and Methods in Dealing with Offenders. Philadelphia: Pennsylvania Valley Publishers, Inc., 1949.

Reith, Charles. The Blind Eye of History. London: Faber and Faber, Limited, 26 Russel Square.

Sarkin, Theodore R. "Role Theory," in Gardner Lindzey (ed.), Handbook of Social Psychology, Vol. I. Cambridge: Addison Wesley Co., 1954.

Shultz, William J. The Humane Movement in the United States, 1910-1922. New York: Columbia University Press, 1924.

Smith, Bruce. Police Systems in the United States. New York: Harper and Brothers, Publishers, 1949.

Sutherland, Robert L., and Julian L. Woodward. Introductory Sociology. New York: Lippincott, 1940.

Verniger, Chester G. Parent and Child. Stanford: Stanford University Press, 1936.

Webster's New International Dictionary, Second Edition, 1957.

Young, Kimball. Social Psychology. New York: Appleton-Century, 1956.

Ananiecki, Florian. The Social Role of Man of Knowledge. New York: Columbia University Press, 1940.

Articles

Alexander, Paul W. "What's This About Punishing Parents," Federal Probation, March 1948, pp. 23-29.

Beck, Bertram. "Protective Casework Revitalized," Child Welfare, November 1955, pp. 1-7.

Brumbaug, Olive. "Protective Services--Whose Responsibility," Child Welfare, April 1953, pp. 13-14.

Buxbaum, Edith. "The Problem of Separation and the Feeling of Identity," Child Welfare, November 1955, pp. 8-15.

Carstens, C.C. "The Development of Social Work for Child Protection," The Annals of the National Conference of Social Work, 1924. Chicago: University of Chicago Press, p. 136.

_____. "A Community Program in the Care of Neglected Children," Proceedings of the National Conference of Social Work, 1920. p. 139.

_____. "The Next Steps in the Work of Child Protection," The Annals of the American Academy of Political and Social Sciences, Vol. XCVIII (November 1921), p. 135.

Cottrell, Leonard S. "Roles and Marital Adjustments," Publications of the American Sociological Society, 27 May 1943, p. 107.

Gordon, Henrietta L. "Criminal Neglect of Children--Who is Guilty?" Child Welfare, February 1953, p. 10.

Hancock, Claire R. "Protective Services for Children," Child Welfare, March 1949, p.4.

Hubbard, Ray S. "Child Protection," Social Work Yearbook, 1929. New York: Russell Sage Foundation, p. 66.

Meier, Elizabeth G. "Interrelationship of Social Causes and Casework in Child Welfare," Social Casework, March 1950, pp. 105-112.

Schour, Esther. "I Believe in Parents," Child Welfare, May 1956, pp. 7-10.

Milliher, Rhoda. "The Police and the Children in Trouble," Federal Probation, March 1955, pp. 26-27.

Neiman, Lionel J., and James W. Huges. "The Problem of the Concept of Role," Social Forces, December 1951, pp. 141-149.

Norman, Sherwood. "Emergency Services in Child Welfare," Child Welfare, April 1954, p. 3.

Scherer, Lorena. "Protective Casework Service," Children, January-February 1956.

Keith-Lucas, Alan. "Social Work and the Court in the Protection of Children," Child Welfare, July 1949, pp. 3-6.

Studt, Elliot, "An Outline for Study of Social Authority Factors in Casework," Child Welfare, June 1954, p. 233.

Swanson, Lynn D. "Police and Children," The Police Chief, June 1958, p. 22.

_____. "Role of the Police in the Protection of Children from Neglect and Abuse," Federal Probation, March 1961, p. 63.

Van Winkle, Mina. "The Policewomen," Proceedings of the National Conference of Social Work. Chicago: The University of Chicago Press, 1926.

_____. "Standardization of Aims and Methods of Work of Policewomen," Proceedings of the National Conference of Social Work (Chicago: Roger and Hall, 1919).

Wells, Alice. "Policewomen of Los Angeles, California," Proceedings of the National Conference of Charities and Corrections. Chicago: The hildmann Printing Co., 1915.

_____. "The Policewoman's Movement--Present Status and Future Needs," Proceedings of the National Conference of Charities and Corrections. Chicago: The Hildmann Printing Co., 1916.

Reports, Pamphlets, and Unpublished Theses

American Humane Association. Forty-Seventh Annual Report of the American Humane Association, 1923. Boston: American Humane Association, 1924, p. 4.

_____. Suggested Language for Legislation on Child Protective Services. A Report of National Agencies Workshop on Child Protective Service, Part II. Denver, Colorado: Children's Division, The American Humane Association, 1958.

American Public Welfare Association. "Preventive and Protective Services to Children, A Responsibility of the Public Welfare Agence." (Summary of material presented by participants in an Institute) Chicago: March 1958.

Allen, Dorothy Frances. "Changing Emphasis in Protective Services to the Child." Unpublished Master's thesis, School of Social Work, University of Southern California, 1943.

Barnett, Eugene W. "A Survey of Ten Families Whose Children Were Emergently Placed by the Police in Subsidized Foster Homes." Unpublished Master's thesis. School of Social Work, University of Southern California, 1961.

California, State of. Department of Social Welfare. A Guide to Protective Services for Children. Sacramento, 1958. (Pamphlet).

Davis, Annie Lee. Children Living in Their Own Home. Washington, D.C.: Children's Bureau, U. S. Government Printing Office, 1953. (Pamphlet.)

De Francis, Vincent. Community Cooperation for Better Child Protection. Denver: Children's Division, The American Humane Association, 1959. (Pamphlet.)

_____. Interpreting Child Protective Services to Your Community. Denver: Children's Division, The American Humane Association, 1957. (Pamphlet.)

_____. Special Skills in Child Protective Services. Denver: Children's Division, The American Humane Association, 1958. (Pamphlet.)

Hamlett, Alice and Joan Overturf. "Protective Services of the Police." Unpublished Master's thesis, School of Social Work, University of Southern California, 1958.

Hancock, Claire R. Protective Services in Practice. Child Welfare League of America, 1948. (Pamphlet.)

Harding, Willie A. "Protective Services for Children: An Annotated Bibliography." Unpublished Master's thesis, School of Social Work, University of Southern California, 1956.

Lt. M. R. Hibbard. "Working Together to Curtail Crime and Delinquency." Unpublished paper presented at the Utah Welfare Meeting, December 1960.

Kahn, Alfred J. "Police and Children." A Study of New York City's Juvenile Aid Bureau. New York: Citizens' Committee on Children of New York City, Inc., 1951. (Mimeographed.)

Mulford, Robert M. *Emotional Neglect of Children.* Denver: Children's Division, The American Humane Association, 1958. (Pamphlet.)

U. S. Department of Health, Education and Welfare. *Child Welfare Services: How They Help Children and Parents.* Children's Bureau Publication No. 359, 1957. (Pamphlet.)

_____. *Four Decades of Action for Children.* Children's Bureau Publication No. 358, 1956. (Pamphlet.)

_____. *Police Services for Juvenile.* Children's Bureau Publication No. 334, 1954. (Pamphlet.)

White House Conference on Child Health and Protection. *Dependent and Neglected Children.* A report of the Committee on Socially Handicapped. New York: D. Appleton-Century Company, 1933.